The Adventures and Inventions of Stewart Blacker

The Adventures and Inventions of Stewart Blacker

Soldier, Aviator, Weapons Inventor

An autobiography
edited by

Barnaby Blacker

Pen & Sword
MILITARY

First published in Great Britain in 2006
Reprinted in 2014 by
Pen & Sword Military
an imprint of
Pen & Sword Books Ltd
47 Church Street
Barnsley
South Yorkshire
S70 2AS

A CIP catalogue record for this book is available from the
British Library

Typeset in 11/13 Sabon by
Lamorna Publishing Services.

Printed and bound by CPI Group (UK) Ltd, Croydon, CR0 4YY

For a complete list of Pen & Sword titles please contact
PEN & SWORD BOOKS LIMITED
47 Church Street, Barnsley, South Yorkshire, S70 2AS, England
E-mail: enquiries@pen-and-sword.co.uk
Website: www.pen-and-sword.co.uk

Contents

Foreword

by

Brian Blacker

My father, Stewart Blacker, was far from being an ordinary man. It would not be quite true to call him an eccentric, but when he passed his Staff College examinations, his examiners were obliged to say 'we are unable to classify this officer'.

His almost pathological hatred of officialdom and what he called 'the abominable no-men of Whitehall', was only matched by his admiration for the martial races of the north-west of the Indian sub-continent.

He was originally a classical scholar, but after many years of soldiering turned his hand to the more practical uses of engineering. When asked where he had developed this skill, he would reply enigmatically, 'by rule of thumb'.

He was a man of striking military appearance, inherited from a long line of Ulster protestants, all of whose sons appear to have entered either the Church or military service. Although he omits to mention the fact, he married in 1927 Doris Peel, daughter of Lord Peel, then Secretary of State for India; they had twin sons and two daughters.

He led an adventurous and hazardous life to the end of his days. Before The First World War he acquired one of the earliest pilots' licences. During the war he flew as an aerial gunnery spotter and was shot down several times, on one occasion breaking his neck - the fifth cervical vertebra - which was the reason his collar size was 18.

After the end of that war he found himself back in the Indian army in that distinguished regiment Queen Victoria's Own Corps of Guides, fighting, with great relish, the armed rabbles of the Bolshevik army in Central Asia, in Persia, Afghanistan, and Kurdistan.

My father was fluent in seven of the tribal languages of the northwest frontier, and spoke Pushtu literally like a native, as instanced by the following tale. On a weekend's shooting leave from Quetta Staff College he was given an escort of local Levies. One evening they were sitting around a roaring fire all chatting together, when one of the Levies turned and said:

'I know who you are.'

'Who am I?' he replied.

'You are one of those Yusufzais,' said the youth, 'I can tell it by the way you talk.'

I still have in my posession the hoof of Marushka, the mare that carried my father some 9,000 miles across Transcaspia and Afghanistan. I have also the badges of rank of a major general of the Red Army, offered to Blacker with an invitation to him to take command of a Bolshevik Division. He accepted the badges, but turned down the invitation.

When he had retired from the army he conceived the idea in 1933 of flying over Mount Everest. His experiences from the First World War perfectly qualified him as navigator and photographer for this expedition.

Following the adventure of the Mount Everest flight, my father concentrated his attention on the greatly needed and much neglected military requirement for anti-tank weapons, foreshadowed by the experience, twenty years earlier, in the fields of Flanders. The recognition of this urgent need manifested itself in the development of the Blacker Bombard and its successor the PIAT. One of my own cherished memories of those days, in the late 1930s, is of being sent out to retrieve the missiles, fired into a neighbouring meadow, at sixpence at time.

But it was at the time that these weapons were being developed that his frustration caused by the intransigence of the 'experts' of the Ordnance Board and other bodies, incapable of realizing their significance, was at its worst. It eventually took the vision of Winston Churchill himself to order their mass production; sadly, too late to combat the Nazi invasion of Poland or the Blitzkrieg of 1940. As he ruefully comments at the end of his book, how different history might have been.

Glossary

Central Powers - the alliance of Germany and Austria-Hungary which fought against Britain, France and Russia in the First World War.

Guides, Queen Victoria's Own Corps of Guides (Lumsdens's) - special troops of the Punjab Frontier Force, based at Mardan in North-West Pakistan – the SAS of the Indian Army – to which Blacker was gazetted as 2nd Lieutenant in April 1909.

Hind, The Army of - The (British) Indian Army.

John Company - The (British) Indian Army.

Keating's powder - Thomas Keating's flea powder.

Loophole - A gunslit.

Mensheviks - Russian political party, anti-capitalist and anti-Bolshevik. They opposed revolution, favouring instead gradual transition to Socialism. For much of the time the Mensheviks were the governing party in Ashkhabad.

Nagaïka - Russian whip.

PIAT - Projector Infantry Anti-Tank; the only British weapon of the Second World War which could be handled by one man on foot and defeat any enemy tank. 115,000 were made and 8,000,000 rounds of ammunition supplied.

Picquet - lookout.

Piffer - soldier of the Punjab Frontier Force.

Point - a few men, usually two, who walk ahead of the main body of men, in order to keep a lookout and give warning of ambush.

Punjab Frontier Force - one of the four armies which made up the Indian Army.

Sangar - a stone breast-work or a small fort.

Sap - a tunnel or trench, built by a sapper.

Soviet - Bolshevik local governing body.

Stuka - the German dive-bomber which brought terror, with its screaming sound and accurate bombing.

Very flame - the flare invented by Samuel Very. Fired into the air from a pistol, it burned for forty seconds, and was used both as a signal and to illuminate the enemy's positions at night.

Whites - White Russians, anti-Bolsheviks.

Yusufzai - a tribe of the North-West Frontier of Pakistan, from which many of the Guides were recruited.

Indian Army Ranks

Risaldar - cavalry officer equivalent to Captain.

Risaldar Major - the most senior Risaldar of the Regiment.

Subadar - infantry officer equivalent to Captain.

Jemadar - officer equivalent to Lieutenant.

Wurdi-Major - assistant to the adjutant of the regiment.

Dafadar-Major - equal to a Regimental Sergeant Major

Havildar - infantry NCO equivalent to Sergeant.

Naik - infantry NCO equivalent to Corporal.

Sepoy - infantry rank equivalent to Private.

Sowar - cavalry rank equivalent to Trooper.

Chapter 1

MEDITERRANEAN MEMORIES

In 1893 I was six years old and in Gibraltar, where our family spent some few years, quartered in the Moorish Castle. My father was Captain of the two stupendous 100-ton guns; they were muzzle-loaders and by then out-of-date, but the firing of them was a tremendous event. After firing, they would clean out the gun chambers by means of a small trumpeter who was pushed up the hydraulic rammer with a rope around his ankles.

From this Castle we could look across to the Queen of Spain's Chair, 1,500 feet high and 6,400 yards away, from which Her Majesty Queen Isabella had watched the great siege in 1786. She vowed she would remain there until the Spanish flag flew over the Rock. Unfortunately for the Spanish forces, this took a very long time; so much so that the unfortunate monarch was unable to change her undergarments for many days. However the governor courteously lowered the Union Jack for long enough for Her Majesty to descend and don another camisole.

A most memorable episode of our stay in the Mediterranean was a party on board that magnificent battleship HMS *Victoria*, not long before she was rammed by the *Camperdown*. The *Victoria* was a remarkable ship for her time, as she mounted huge guns which were breech-loaders and of 16.25 inches calibre. By some extraordinary aberration, however, these guns, and the somewhat lighter guns in other ships, were not mounted in turrets but in barbettes, with no overhead cover, making the crews vulnerable to the fire of the smaller pieces of the enemy. No doubt an official committee decided that.

Later, HMS *Victoria* ran aground on an outlying part of the

1

Island of Malta. Admiral Tryon, a very large and well-nourished person, was fussing around the forecastle, during the efforts to get her off, when he fell overboard. The ribald sailors later asserted that the tidal wave which he occasioned actually floated her off.

While at Gibraltar we went on a memorable jaunt to Granada and Seville. The train to Granada took all day as on board was the famous bull fighter Mazzantini and at every station the people flocked to see him. At Ronda, the cradle of bull fighting, the dead horses from the ring were thrown into the gorge where they were eaten by eagles.

From the Mediterranean we came back to Gibraltar and embarked for home in a remarkable vessel of Queen Victoria's Navy, namely the *Himalaya*. She was square rigged with three masts, but being a barque had no square sails on her mizzen. She had been built during the Crimean War, with a steam engine, so that she could supply reinforcements quickly to that ill-omened peninsula. Her engine was a somewhat primitive contraption, working its steam from the pressure of fourteen pounds per square inch, and soon it broke down.

The Commanding Officer, Sir Edward Chichester, possessed a strong dislike for steam engines, and therefore placed his Chief Engineer under close arrest and confined him to his cabin, on a charge of allowing the engine to break down. This he was entitled to do, the Chief Engineer of those days being a Warrant Officer. The Captain knew that no one else except the Chief Engineer could make the engines go, so by confining him to his cabin he was able to sail all the way to Plymouth, which took a fortnight. This was an ever-memorable experience, as we sailed with fresh winds behind us and the towering masses of flax canvas and the wide-spreading yards above us, sustained by their hemp rigging and handled by a hundred or so bearded topmen.

She was armed with fourteen Armstrong 12-pounder guns on a broadside. The captain of the aftermost gun told me all about his pet piece of ordnance. He had the pipe-clayed lanyard very neatly coiled on top of the breech block, and I remember my disbelief in the possibility of firing a gun otherwise than by supplying a flaming portfire from a linstock. However, he convinced me that there were such modern things as friction tubes and lanyards.

When we got into the Bay of Biscay, much to everybody's

surprise and indeed joy, we fell in with a Norwegian full-rigged sailing ship which appeared to be derelict. We closed with her. She was a remarkable sight; her bulwarks were stoved in but, apparently as she was laden with wood, she continued to float, kept fairly dry by a strange windmill which Norwegian Maritime Law insisted on their ships carrying between the fore and main masts. This worked a pump which kept the water out of the hold.

The sailors were overjoyed at the sight, and painted themselves pictures of well-earned salvage and something to rattle about in their pockets after the Admiralty Court had done with her. They pulled over to the Norwegian, confirmed that she was indeed a derelict, and took her in tow. All went well that day and night and the next day; but that evening a great commotion arose on deck. It appeared that the derelict had taken a sudden dive, perhaps because of the pull of the hawser on her foremast. Quartermasters seized the huge axes hanging at the stern and commenced heaving at the hawser to cut it and save the *Himalaya* from following her down beneath the waves. The captain danced like a cat on hot bricks over the wire rope which the sailor kept missing in the dark until my father suggested a light. Ladies were fainting in the saloon until we could assure them all was clear.

In due course we sailed into Plymouth Sound under the guns of the Breakwater and the Bovisand Forts. These two strongholds were just on the point of being re-armed with breech-loaders to replace their antiquated muzzle-loaders. My scholastic career was about to begin.

Chapter 2

BECOMING A SOLDIER

After a couple of years in Gibraltar, my father was promoted to command the forts and guns at the entrance to Plymouth Sound. From there, in 1899, fate wafted me first to a happy school at Westgate, then with a grim bellypinch to a sordid house at Cheltenham. It took a broken and neglected football ankle to rescue me from this situation. I was delivered to Dublin into the hands of a most kind and skilful surgeon, Sir William Thompson, and so off my crutches.

My mobility restored, study had to be resumed for the Army, if possible the Army of Hind. This spelled Bedford, with its really first-rate tradition both scholastically, and with the rugger ball and the oar.

Good luck put me under two of those very rare birds, efficient schoolmasters, one being the famous Sanderson (H.K.St.J. Sanderson), the other the almost idolized 'Rob' (T.P. Gorden Robinson). At this time one Bernard Law Montgomery was Captain of Rugby at St. Paul's. He omits to mention in his memoirs that in 1905 we beat them by 64 points to nil; indeed we allowed no school to score a single point against us. On the river in that year we beat Shrewsbury, even after our 13-stone No. 5 had broken the blade off his oar.

I was still not up to rugby at this level, so my winter months inclined towards the ballistic art. Eventually four of us, including a future Bishop of Gloucester, constructed a very gratifying mortar. We had been stimulated by what the Japanese had achieved in their trench-to-trench fights against the Russians in Port Arthur and 203-metre Hill, in which the light, simple, highly-manoeuvrable bamboo-reinforced mortar had played no small part. This we imitated with good English ash, bound like theirs with steel wire. Lindsay Ritchie, the brain of the syndicate, built it around a croquet ball. Though it has not much ballistic coefficient, a croquet ball is beautifully spherical, true to diameter, and with a good sectional density, so this was a very logical choice of projectile. (In various small ways we anticipated those jam-tin mortars which we later built for ourselves in Flanders, when the bulging brain of Lord Haldane and his Strulbrugs had overlooked such trifling details).

We made screws of black powder in cigarette papers, measuring each out in empty cartridge cases. After several trials great triumph came. The projectile soared up over three hundred yards and made its impact in the headmaster's greenhouse. This caused alarums and excursions, but as no headmaster could imagine that a boy could hurl a croquet ball even as much as thirty yards, so the search was restricted to that radius, and we escaped punishment.

Sandhurst was the next objective. The Army Council, following that well-known adage that there are two British Armies, one that is always being re-organized, and one that goes on parade, re-organized the entrance qualification to Sandhurst. This involved bringing science into the examination.

The main chemistry examination was practical and held in a vast laboratory in South Kensington. Here we formed up, each in front of a section of teak bench covered with weird bottles and appliances, and beheld a mysterious pill-box containing a fine black powder. I mixed some of it with each of the noxious fluids from the jars before me: still no result; so in desperation I put some of the stuff into a hollow carbon block and turned a blow-pipe flame on to it. The result surpassed my wildest forecast. Great showers of sparks filled nearly the whole apartment. My examinee comrades turned all sorts of queer colours, whilst the invigilator rushed at me with a raucous demand to 'take that to the stink cupboard'. But I refused to have my own examination compromised, foreseeing that if I did not get any marks, neither would anybody else. This thought made me impervious to the fumes; I considered that any rival who had actually studied chemistry was behaving unfairly. In the end, all turned out happily so far as my own marks were concerned.

Sandhurst was quite a quaint place to look back upon. We no longer drilled in blue serge jackets but in khaki, and on Saturdays and Sundays donned tunics of fine scarlet cloth just like the Foot Guards. Each of our six companies had a Regular Staff Sergeant Instructor, who never used bad language but was quite able to deal with the Gentleman Cadet without it.

For the first few weeks the drill was certainly tough. Heaven only knows what would have happened to the cadet who let his rifle fall from frozen fingers. At the end of a year, averaging barely one hour's infantry drill a day, we were the best drilled battalion in the Army, and one of the best shooting ones.

Not everything went perfectly all the time. On one Saturday ceremonial parade, with us all in scarlet tunics and with the Colour party, we were forming up into a line from a column. An order miscarried, and half the Company turned the wrong way. Momentary confusion resulted, and the Second-in-Command, taking the parade, said what he thought:

'Did I say "right incline", Sergeant Major?'

'You said "right incline", Sir.'

'You're a liar,' said our Staff Sergeant, but just too loud. So he went into arrest.

Next day, Orderly Room proceedings were held in camera, so that the ribaldry of the Gentleman Cadets should receive no cheer. Naturally an Orderly Room clerk overheard, and passed on to the waiting masses, that the Staff Sergeant, to avoid scandal, had been told to apologize to the Sergeant Major. The report transmitted by the eavesdropper was, 'Sergeant Major, I called you a liar. It's as you were.'

Infantry drill in those days, indeed all through the 1914 war, contained much of the archaic, from Frederic William of Prussia modified by Sir John Moore. When one drilled a Company, for example, one had never to forget which was the front rank and which the rear – there were only two ranks, which formed into fours to march in column. It was a terrific gaffe to finish up with one's Company in line with its rear rank in front. This dated back to the days when the infantry soldier fought front rank kneeling

6

and rear rank standing, usually to beat off the cavalry attack. The design of our boots also owed its origin to this tactic. The front rank man had perforce to kneel, and for this reason his boot had to have a very stiff, thick clumped sole, otherwise his toes would become paralysed from cramp. The Quartermaster General's branch of the War Office continued to supply this pattern of boot long after the need for it had disappeared.

A great deal, and perhaps the most valuable part, of our outdoor work lay in mapping the neighbourhood, because making a map really taught one to read it.

The most welcome part, however, was our cavalry instruction, which took us up to the stage of riding as one of a squadron of mounted infantry. We carried sword and rifle, for which one seemed to need at least three hands. Luckily we were spared the lance, for which yet another hand would have been needed. The horses provided were by no means fire-snorting Pegasuses, but they carried us about cheerfully over the Chobham ridges and such like blasted heaths.

The culmination was the riding examination at the end of the last term over numerous jumps. My steed took me over all these with aplomb, except for the last, which had a damp ditch on the offside. She, being a mare, decided to remain on the wrong side and to project me head first into the said ditch at the feet of the examining officer, who was no less than the great Baden-Powell himself, at whom, at the crucial moment, she winked. However, all was well. He made one feel, in his most charming way, that this was quite the most usual thing in the world, entirely undeserving of comment. In fact, he gave me quite good marks, so no wonder his juniors were devoted to him.

The teaching at Sandhurst was mostly pretty sound, except of course in the handling of weapons. The British Army's weapons in the recently-ended South African War were, it is almost needless to say, obsolete and outclassed by the Boers'. Our tactical instruction was even more out of date, even though we sat with some reverence at the feet of our officers, the heroes of that conflict. We possessed one 15-pounder field gun, now very, very much behind the times, but not a single machine gun. In fact we were told almost nothing about them, except what we gleaned from the battle reminiscences of the Staff Sergeants.

From Sandhurst I contrived to pass out with enough marks to attain the Army which had, since 1886, been called the Indian Army. This gave great pleasure to the family, of which many sons had served in the older Armies of 'John Company'. In fact seven brothers and cousins out of fourteen from a single generation had been killed in action, mainly in our tough wars of Hindustan.

For the first year of my service, as was customary in the Indian Army, I was attached to a British regiment, the Royal Irish Fusiliers. My company Commander was Charles Conyers, whom I was to see killed at St Eloi eight years later.

Chapter 3

PATHANS, EDUCATION
AND TOM MIX

On the voyage to India an execrable gunner major organized a
boxing tournament and humbugged another second lieutenant
and myself to give what he craftily called 'three exhibition
rounds'. What with the heat of 'tween decks in the Red Sea and
the yells of the excited soldiery, these developed into a bloody
contest and I joined the Regiment with a really ripe black eye. A
few days earlier, Charles Conyers sustained a similar injury to the
left eye in a guest night for the entertainment of the 14th
Ferozepore Sikhs. Ranks of sergeant and below considered these
adornments in their officers to be eminently right and proper.

Regimental guest nights could certainly be rousing affairs, especially when a national patron saint was being commemorated.
The Fusiliers, I recall, celebrated St Patrick's night in due form.
One of our guests was the Garrison Chaplain, who made his
adieus in the early hours of the morning under a brilliant frosty
Punjab moon. To the farewells of all he climbed into his dog cart,
whip in hand. With his man in the back seat he drove off, cheered
by his hosts, up the great, wide, tree-lined Mall. However, the
little horse yawed sharply to starboard, and then to port. Zigs and
zags repeated themselves with progressively increasing amplitude.
Before very long the dog cart subsided into the ditch. Willing
hands rushed forward, lifted it out of the mud, put the little horse
on its feet, replaced the whip in the parson's hand and him on the
box, and started the shandrydan off again. More zigs and zags
followed, and this time the stranding took place in the other

ditch; once more the chaplain was salvaged and sent on his way. This time, however, his man spotted the fact that some humorist had crossed the reins under the chin of the sober but flummoxed pony.

In 1908 we left the Punjab and proceeded to Jandola in Waziristan. Thirty years earlier, the Wild West had been almost a fun fair in comparison with that rough, tough country. The Waziri was at heart a very jolly fellow, and quite a sportsman. However he had strong feelings about bureaucrats and tax gatherers, and was only too willing to be egged on by militant ecclesiastics, known as mullahs, to shoot at policemen and soldiers. When, on the other hand, we got the Wazir and his cousin, the Mahsud, really on our side, as in the frontier levies and regiments of the Indian Army and as in Flanders in 1915, he did us proud.

Particularly playful were the inhabitants of the Buner and Black Mountain area north of Peshawur. In 1857 the Bengal Native Infantry mutinied, and were pursued, many to their deaths, by John Nicholson, Commissioner in Peshawur. At nightfall the scattered survivors slunk off into the high, rugged mountains of Buner. For generations after, the descendants of these Hindustanis made a tough, hard core of fanaticism.

One such was Multan Khan, who also provides an interesting example of the relationship of education to fighting value. He had enlisted in the 20th Punjab Infantry, and by 1903 had risen to the dignity of two stripes on his arm, without acquiring any book learning.

About that time, under Lord Kitchener's influence, an elaborate series of educational tests had been instituted which all regiments had to undergo. Multan Khan did not show up very well in the limelight which played on him and the section under his command. The results of his endeavours seemed to harmonize less and less with the ideal depicted by the General Staff. Matters came to a head and Multan was invited to present himself before his Colonel to show why he should not lose his stripes as being unworthy to command a section, or rather to perform the various parlour tricks that were expected of a section commander at that time. The upshot was that he was invited to remove himself from the regiment and return to civilian life, the reasons shown on one of the multifarious Army forms being 'lack of initiative, power of command and tactical ability'.

Multan shook the dust of the gritty parade ground from his feet, disposed of His Majesty's uniform, and returned quietly but thoughtfully to his rocky mountain home.

In due course his thoughts shaped themselves into a desire to demonstrate, by practical means, that the ideas of the General Staff as regards fighting efficiency were not altogether sound. In a word, he became a raider, gathering to himself a band of about thirty choice and enterprising spirits, each armed with a modern rifle.

He encountered far more success as the commander of this organization of his own than he had in the regular infantry. By sheer merit he hacked and shot his way to fame, until in a very short time he had achieved the pinnacle of his ambitions and was universally acclaimed by all alike as being the scourge of the Peshawar frontier and at the top of his new profession.

His most remarkable and meritorious feat was one of several raids which he carried out on Peshawar itself. This city was surrounded by a wall about thirty feet high, pierced by a dozen or so massive gates fitted with steel loopholes – gunslits – on each of which was stationed a police guard armed with rifles and in telephone communication with a central reserve, who lay under arms all night.

Multan commenced operations, as he often did, by announcing in a courteously worded missive to the Political Department the precise date and hour of his intended raid. To the minute, he attacked and over-powered the police post on one side of the gates, whose attention had been distracted by a carefully pre-arranged disturbance within. The main body of his gang then proceeded to the street of the money-lenders, whose abode lay in a narrow alley forming a cul-de-sac with a blank wall at one end. Needless to say it was by way of the blank wall that Multan made his entry, a hole having been dug through it the night before.

The police reserve found itself in pursuit of two other parties, who led them a chase through the tortuous ways of the city, till at last – so the police thought – they were brought to bay. The police found themselves firing in the dark, down a narrow street, at opponents who returned their fire with briskness and determination. It was not until this duel had been in progress for some time that the police discovered that they were firing at each other, Multan's associates having led them to opposite ends of the alley, and then vanished.

This little fight, together with the recriminations which ensued, occupied some time. Meanwhile, Multan's own party had been passing smartly from the house of one money-lender to another, filling up their sacks as they went.

Long before the confusion had been straightened out, Multan's mules, once the property of His Majesty, were well on their way to the hills laden with gold and silver.

By dawn the troops had been turned out and, acting on information received – and obligingly supplied by the hirelings of Multan – spent a long night out in the open in cold, wet ditches, safeguarding a line far remote from Multan Khan.

Multan eventually came to his end – as all raiders do – when he encountered a foeman worthy of his steel, then a Captain in the Frontier Force. The Political Department had at last succeeded in installing an informer as a member of Multan's band. The raider lay up with about thirty rifles on a little rocky hillock ten miles south of Peshawur.

The information came into the hands of the Squadron Leader of the 19th Lancers, who took his squadron to the appointed spot and, dashing soldier as he was, put them at it at a gallop. Unfortunately, he himself had an awkward habit of being hit by the first bullet in every fight and an early shot from Multan brought him to the ground. His second-in-command, a lad from Sandhurst, was no more fortunate, as his horse was killed and he was knocked unconscious through landing on his head. Several of the squadron were hit, and as the ground was too rocky for the horses to move, the survivors dismounted and resorted to a fire fight with their rifles. They were eventually compelled to send for outside aid, which arrived shortly in the shape of a double-company of the 59th Punjab Infantry.

The Company Commander, a well-tried frontier officer (a cousin of mine) took his men along at the double, and arrived to the aid of the cavalry. They outflanked the little hillock; there was a fresh burst of fire, bayonets were fixed, and a few moments later Multan's gallant, if illegal, career came to its not unworthy end.

Most of his men were killed where they stood, Multan himself despatching a man whilst at his last gasp; but half a dozen or so recovered sufficiently of their wounds in Peshawar Civil Hospital to be hanged with all the formality of Bumbledom in Peshawar jail.

So ended Multan's practical exposition of the value of book learning to a leader of men.

There was another occasion when the young men of Buner got somewhat above themselves. It was ascribed by some to the cinema, which appeared for the very first time in Nowshera, their market town, where they had come in from the mountains for shopping. Tom Mix, or someone like him, demonstrated the technique by which bad men in ten-gallon hats could secure for themselves the contents of the safe in the express car of their weekly train. It all seemed so simple that the men of Buner said to themselves, 'Why do we not go and do likewise?'

So, sure enough, they worked out the time at which the express from Rawalpindi was to stop for water at a convenient wayside halt not far east of Nowshera. They also made enquiry about the day on which the safe with the railwaymen's monthly salaries would be in the baggage car.

At midnight, as the huge broad gauge express engine slowed down to the water tower, a score of rifle shots rang out. The European engine driver fell in the first volley, and a moment later a gang of Buneris burst into the guard's van to break open the safe. The Pathan station watchman fell dead, whilst a few British officers in the train who had guns sprang up from their bunks to exchange shots. The safe was empty, and the Buner men vanished into the midnight darkness. They had picked the right day, but by some chance the railway's cashier had put his pay back by twenty-four hours. The young men of Buner felt that they had been diddled, that the North Western Railway had not played the game, and that their cinema entrance money had been wasted.

However, at Attock, where the railway comes into the Frontier Province across the Indus, the stationmaster was a Hindu. That in itself was provocation, so they worked out a plan and kidnapped him. Then they sent to the headquarters of that section of the railway a courteously-worded request for a ransom, on what they felt to be reasonable terms.

There was no precedent in the railway world for this, because Pathans of British territory had tended to consider the North Western Railway as part of their own world, even though they did not always hold with paying for tickets. The North Western Railway was state-owned, and therefore a demand for a ransom, for which there was no precedent, upset their civil service minds very much indeed. The bureaucratic processes went on for weeks and weeks, punctuated by regular requests, couched in phrases of courtly, classical Persian, for that ever-growing ransom. Suddenly the flow ceased, and the Traffic Manager put away his fat file with a sigh.

The spring weather began to warm up, and some railway men hovering about a goods siding observed a locked wagon with no address on it and a certain aura about it. It was forced open. Inside were a score of those four-gallon tins usually employed for kerosene; neatly distributed in them were twenty sections of the missing Hindu stationmaster. Buner patience had become exhausted.

I had more dealings with the Buner a few years later, but before then I enjoyed a change of scene and occupation.

Chapter 4

INTO THE AIR

Officers in India got not only three months leave every year, but in every fourth year a long furlough of eight or twelve months, enough for a passage home. The latter first came my way in 1911, the year after Monsieur Blériot had inoculated us with the aviation bug. So it was not long before I formed up at Brooklands for my first flight.

The Marquess of Tullibardine had done a good deal at his own expense at Blair Atholl to help with Army flying. Needless to say Whitehall took a cross-eyed view of it. I have filed away a letter from Army Headquarters saying that the Government of India did not recognize such a thing. However both British and Indian Armies owned balloons, although that of the latter had been devoured by white ants some years before. At Farnborough, the Royal Engineers struggled pathetically with gas-bags of goldbeater's skin; with Samuel Cody's hair-raising man-lifting kite; and with tiny airships. In 1911, eight years after the Wrights, public nagging forced the addition of an aeroplane Company to the lighter-than-air Company. This company had two officers of the Royal Engineers, Reginald Cammell and Bertie Reynolds, the former of whom possessed his own Blériot XI bis with two side-by-side seats.

For some odd bureaucratic reason anyone who was not of the RE had to qualify as a pilot. This meant that he had to take the Royal Aero Club's 'brevet', at his own expense, and then apply to be attached to this newly-hatched Air Battalion.

The old pre-Kaiser Army was run very much at the expense of

15

its officers' pockets, but even so the £75 that this brevet was going to cost was a grim shock to this junior officer's financial reserves and to his bank manager's nerves. This was all the more so when the cost of a passage from Bombay had already dealt swashing blows to both. Fortunately an elderly Hindu called Ramji Lal, who to a great extent financed the entire Corps of Guides, came to the rescue.

The £75 came and was passed to a Brooklands firm of genuine pioneers, who had evolved a beautiful little tractor biplane, much ahead of its time, and a piece of aerodynamic artistry to boot. This was, of course, a single-seater with a tiny water-cooled engine of thirty horsepower. Its radiator lay flat on the top wing, and automatically registered any overheating by boiling over down the back of the pilot's neck.

One's first flight obviously had to be solo. Indeed, it was really only a long hop of a few hundred yards over the smooth sward of Brooklands, yet it was the transcendent vision of a lifetime. For years and years the youth of our generation had dreamed of real flight, dreams fed by 10,000 story writers. Suddenly the brain was dazzled by the realization.

More straight flights, and then ambition truly soared to the accomplishment of what we called a 'circuit'. This was the open sesame to that almost mystical document in its dark blue, smooth leather cover, copper-plate engraving within, gold leaf without, the 'International Brevet'. Much discussion and debate filled the 'Blue Bird' where the aviators gathered. We were a small band, united by the ambition to get confidently into the air, but alas often thrown into dejection by the death of one of that very, very few. No one really knew anything about flying, or rather about airmanship, so when one of the learners became due to hurl himself into his first circuit, he received much advice, all contradictory and much of it wrong.

So, having waited, as we all did, for an almost windless morning, this writer took off in grand and confident style, but with the lamentable notion that when he ruddered to turn back into that green oval he did not need to bank to raise his outer wing. The startling result came in a flash. In a moment the world turned, not quite upside down, but, it seemed, nearly so. The little aircraft floated on its head and on its port wing-tip, less than 100

16

feet above the high concrete of Brooklands track.

When one becomes persuaded that one's demise is momentarily imminent a kind of mesmerism suffuses and freezes the senses. A vivid picture remained burnt into my eyes' memory of a strange circular object just beyond the port wing-tip. It could only have been there for a small fraction of a second, but the memory remained scorched in. It was a telegraph pole seen from above.

Meanwhile the tiny aeroplane recovered itself, almost it seemed, by a miracle. Up came the nose, up came the port wing, down came the tail, and a second later came a smooth landing in the middle of an excited and voluble crowd of those rudimentary airmen. Comment was free and much of the 'I told you so' order from those who had done no such thing. However, the good little aeroplane was intact, so we went on flying until another pupil broke a strut in the wooden undercart.

This stopped all progress, because there was simply no money to buy another. Stung to fury by these delays, I walked into Weybridge, and from a hardware shop purchased an excellent broom handle of fine straight-grained ash for one and sixpence. We soon fixed this into the undercarriage, and so once more had a perfectly good aeroplane.

But luck was soon out for our little band of pupil airmen, because a never-sufficiently-to-be-reviled naval engineer officer bought the machine over our heads. He fitted it with floats and it became a sea plane. This did not console us.

Brooklands had its share of personalities. One was Mrs Maurice Hewlett. When her son applied to join the Naval Air Service, his reply to the official question about where he learned to fly was, 'My mother taught me'. This remark nearly cost him a court martial even before he joined. But it was only the truth; Mrs.Hewlett was the first woman to gain the Royal Aero Club Flying Certificate, in 1911, and directed a flying school in partnership with M. Blondeau at Brooklands from 1910 to 1914.

Another was a fine engineer, Robert McFie, who designed and built his own aeroplane at Fambridge in Essex in 1909, and in 1911 designed a tank. When the proposal reached Whitehall, it was endorsed 'The man's mad'; but later on, in 1915, when we really wanted tanks badly, someone dug out his drawings and the outcome was our Mark I tank. A grateful country gave him and his co-designer Mr Nesfield, an award of £500.

Meanwhile, with no aeroplane and no money, the Brooklands episode came to a halt. But it is wonderful what one can do to raise the wind when all seems lost. That splendid firm, Bristol Aviation, to whom the country owes so much, came to the rescue. Knowing that I had already gone some way, they offered me a chance to qualify at a reduced rate, payable in instalments.

Their school was at Larkhill on Salisbury Plain and run by the great Henri Jullerot assisted by Fleming who, to our great regret, was killed in a spin. The Bristol School had biplanes of the Farman type, with those immortal Gnome engines. They were pushers – that is to say, with the engine behind – so one had to relearn the art of flying on the pusher basis. This was not really very difficult, but I found myself being extremely cautious, having learned at Brooklands not to be too slapdash. As the saying went, it was better to be the oldest aviator than the boldest.

Even so there came one more misadventure, when the Gnome engine cut out just before a landing, on the wrong side of a wire fence. A sheep paid the penalty, and broke the propeller. The broadminded Bristol Company charged me a nominal amount for the new propeller, but the farmer exacted thirty shillings for the sheep.

The Gnome engine was a monument to French engineering genius and to its parents, the brothers Seguin. The whole engine rotated around a stationary and hollow crankshaft, through which it sucked its mixture which came through spring loaded valves, one in the head of each of its seven pistons. The exhaust valves were in the cylinder heads, and were worked by pull rods, these in turn being moved in and out by a strange device called a 'Cam-pack'. This inspired an early RFC pilot, who wrote:

A bold aviator lay dying,
And to his sad comrades did say,
Take the crankshaft out of my kidneys,
Take the con rod out of my brain,
From the small of my back take the Cam-pack,
And assemble the engine again.

Soon the great day of my test arrived. The aeroplane had its new propeller, the judges were ready, and the day was fine. The test had during these few weeks become more difficult. The Fédération Internationale now demanded a figure-of-eight instead of the original plain circuit of one kilometre. The Gnome, however ingenious, brought with it a problem. As the whole weight of the engine revolved at 1,200 rpm, the gyroscopic force generated was no small matter. When one turned to the left it tended to depress the nose; this involved no risk, because it also increased one's flying speed. Contrariwise, if one turned to the right, this gyroscopic force raised the aircraft's nose upwards; this reduced one's speed, and so from lift, of which one had mighty little to spare in those days. Hence there were stalls, and spinning to the ground. Several people were killed until someone hit upon that obscure reason.

The Gnome engine was oiled with castor oil, which had a strange little indicator just in front of one's right hand, a glass inverted dome in which the oil pulsed up and down with each stroke of the pump. When the pilot had sufficient mastery and control of his machine to take his eyes for a moment off the skyline in order to check that the oil really was going up and down, he felt that truly he had progressed indeed.

Those early box-kites possessed a front elevator some ten feet ahead, which kept the machine level with the skyline – though one could seldom afford the luxury of much elevating. To the middle of this, the sagacious airman tied a length of tape; if this blew straight back at him, he knew that he was not side-slipping or skidding. In later degenerate years someone invented an expensive 'turn and bank indicator'.

Anyway, the test was passed, and the Brevet arrived; so it was back to paper work and application to be attached to the new Air Battalion, commanded by Reginald Cammell, he of the twin-seater Blériot. Red tape was unexpectedly minimal, perhaps because the great Herbert Vaughan Cox was Military Secretary at the India Office, but needless to say officialdom insisted that all attachment was to be at the officer's own expense, and at his own risk.

I was to go to the Air Battalion camp outside Cambridge with Bertie Reynolds, who had just been assigned a new Bristol with, imagine it, an eight-cylinder Renault engine, free from that disconcerting centrifugal force of the Gnome which was liable to catch one off one's guard in bumpy weather. What was really startling was that it was fitted with a compass. Here was air navigation indeed, if one had a moment to spare to look at it. We bade farewell to Henri Jullerot, to Adjutant Noel and others, and prepared to go to the great cavalry manoeuvres, which were to be in Cambridgeshire. We intended to fly there, but this new aeroplane decided that it would not lift both of us, so Reynolds flew and I went by train.

At the camp was much excitement – Reynolds was missing. Somewhat dishevelled, he appeared later, minus the aeroplane, and reported his story. He had been flying quite gaily from Larkhill towards Cambridge, when suddenly the machine turned itself upside down, as aeroplanes did in those days for no reason then known. He described to us, his mesmerized listeners, how he found himself hanging, head downwards, by his knees, which were hooked into the undercarriage. The aeroplane, inverted, swooped from here to there in a series of what the scientist afterwards told us we should call 'Phugoid' curves. Bertie's fairy godmother must have been on the *qui vive* that day, because each of these phugoid curves had a sector which was almost flat. During one of these flattish glides the aeroplane must have been struck by the earth near a small river, still upside down.

Our hero, miraculously unharmed, pulled himself together enough to look round and scramble to the earth, and his gaze encountered a stark naked man. A quick deduction told him he must have passed into the next world and that here was an angel who, like himself, now was minus wings. The angel, who was as surprised as the aviator, had merely been for a swim, and soon each explained himself to the other, insisting on his own reality.

We were glad to have Bertie back in one piece, aeroplane or no aeroplane. As the old airman's saying goes: any landing is a good landing that one can walk away from.

After all this, the cavalry manoeuvres were cancelled because of the railway strike; instead we had the great excitement of the *Daily Mail* Circuit of Britain, for which the title of 'Official' and its historic brassard were bestowed on me. The win was a popular one, and went to a charming French naval lieutenant, Jean Conneau, in a Blériot monoplane of primitive type.

My enthusiasm for the air did not fade, in spite of official frowns and scowls. Officer audiences listened with odd and mixed response to one's lectures. Some scouted the bare idea; others were enthralled by a glimpse of the future and of exploits like Pegoud's looping of the loop. Generally the idea was that finance ministers might possibly allow an army to have one or two aeroplanes here and there for the General to see 'what was on the other side of the hill'. The notion of fighting in the air, and that 'hundreds will be used and scores will be crashed', was thought fantastic – the sort of thing that would be said by a naïve junior officer ignorant of the ways of finance departments.

In the fullness of time my attachment to the Air Battalion came to an end, and I returned to regimental duty in India with the Guides.

It is worth recording that this was the year of the great Delhi Durbar. The enterprising Maharaja of Patiala purchased a Bristol biplane in order to have it flown there. Here seemed an opportunity for me to get into the air again, but fate intervened in the form of one of the Maharaja's own officers, who determined to fly it but, alas, merely achieved a collision with a field gun, in which the poor aeroplane came off worst.

Chapter 5

FRONTIER EXCURSIONS

Soon after, back in India, it became my duty to reconnoitre an extension of the network of sites for visual signal stations around the vale of Peshawur. These were for heliographs, because the range of our antique oil-burning lamps was not long enough to be of much use. A badly-needed site was on the summit of the Ambela Pass, which is the pass which leads northward into the Buner portion of the Swat Valley, to which I have previously referred.

It was towards this wild territory that we, that is my half-dozen or so signallers of the Guides cavalry, rode out. We halted at the pleasant village of Hamzakot, of which our own Risaldar Major, the much-loved Khwaja, was the squire. He had his own village levy, armed with Martini rifles supplied by the Government, and he lent me a few of these nimble lads.

We climbed on foot up a narrow stony track, up into thick pine forests, and up again into sparse scrub and rock. In front there sprang up sheer the peak called the Eagle's Nest. On the other side was Crag Picquet, and in between, the col called Kutql Garh, or the place of blood. A glance round, and Lance Dafadar Ratan Chand began to set up his heliograph. Sure enough, in a moment, rifle fire banged out all around us, and I mean all around. Every now and then black-clothed figures appeared from behind boulders, and we shot back at them without sparing our ammunition. These Buner people wore black or very dark blue, which gave them a slightly sinister look.

Soon it dawned on me how it was that loud reports were coming from very close behind us. Explosive bullets were deto-

PAMIRS

Mintaka
Pass)(

AFGHANISTAN

25,425

Chitral

21,295

CHITRAL

21,890

25,370

Hunza

18,750

Gilgit

NAGAR

24,270

Lowarai
Pass

Dir

Kunar R.

Swat River

Indus R.

26,620

KASHMIR

Kabul
R.

Malakand

BUNER

Ambela
Pass

Mardan

PESHAWUR

Nowshera

RAWALPINDI

0 10 20 30 40 50 miles

WAZIRISTAN

Jandola

PUNJAB

nating on the rocks. Though it was a relief to think that we were not surrounded, the prospect of being hit by a detonating bullet rather offset that. The ingenious men of Buner, who at that time mostly possessed Martinis, had hollowed out the noses of those big lead bullets and inserted the detonators used with high explosive. These they had obtained through the usual Pathan sleight of hand from the works of the great canal tunnel then being driven by the British through the granite Malakand range. By the same token their Martinis had come from Australia: when that Government re-armed its troops with the .303 they had sold their Martinis in rather too open a market.

In due course the Buners saw that they would get no change from us, and dribbled away from rock to rock northwards of the Pass into what was incontestably independent territory. We got our signal message through, and with dignity made our way back to Hamzakot, where the Khwaja congratulated us cordially on having beaten off his hereditary adversaries. But the upshot was not quite as simple as that.

A day or two later the Political people reported me to the Chief Commissioner, Sir George Roos-Keppel, for having aggressively invaded Buner. This was most unjust, because we had been careful not to go down the north side of the Pass, whilst the south side was incontestably British. Roos-Keppel was no friend of the Yusufzai, so I shook a little in my boots. Fortunately our divisional General was Sir James Willcocks, a pretty tough character who had not long before conquered Ashanti, stopping the great local sport of mass crucifixions. James 'by the grace of God', as we knew him, stood up for his subordinates, and far from being court-martialled or even having my leave stopped, I received official governmental commendation.

In 1915 the Khwaja appeared in France as senior aide-de-camp to the same Sir James Willcocks, who was commanding the India Corps there.

One way and another, the young Buner men would not keep the peace. The Government, stung to action, decided to punish a delinquent village. So the Nowshera Brigade mounted an offensive, or a counter-raid.

Their commander, Bannantine-Allason, arranged manoeuvres to take place to the north of Nowshera. Movement orders were

24

issued, and umpires detailed and given their white armbands. The Brigade Group moved off in the dark, but soon they realized that their Commander was not leading them to the north, but well to the south; in fact into the foothills of Buner territory. No one could have been more bewildered than some of the umpires, who were invited to take off their white arm bands and to witness the distribution of ball ammunition. The Brigade made its advance, not over the Ambela where the Buner men rather naturally expected it, but over the next pass to the east, called Malandri. By dawn the hills on each flank were duly picqueted with lookout posts, and one infantry battalion and our cavalry of the Guides descended into the valley to surround the offending village. My part was to run the signal communications, and to see that transport convoys functioned properly.

On the summit of the pass, watching the encirclement, stood the General and his Staff. One of the junior officers was his galloper. As some of the fugitives tried to drive away livestock from the village, that livestock which the political people meant to confiscate, the mountain battery burst a few deterrent rounds of shrapnel over them.

While all this was going on, someone noticed big clouds of smoke coming from some copses to the left front of headquarters. 'Why,' said someone, 'are the Gunners firing black powder and not cordite?'

'The battery is not there,' said someone else, 'they are just to our right and they *are* firing cordite.'

So our junior subaltern made his way into the thicket to investigate the phenomenon. A moment later the brushwood was torn by a sort of cyclonic disturbance, leaves and branches flew, and horrid language came out. Ready hands came to help, and found our young officer locked in a death struggle with a very old Buner with a long white beard, who had been assiduously discharging an equally ancient matchlock at the General ever since daybreak, but with no luck. No one had the heart to be unkind to the old gentleman, who seemed to be actuated by purely patriotic motives, so he was merely detained, as the magistrates would say, 'until the rising of the court'. He tottered away, after paying his respects to our General, no doubt in time for lunch. The Politicals got their prisoners and some cattle, and we all went home.

One of my several roles was Station Staff Officer, and so when a Hindi contractor was suspected of supplying adulterated flour, it was to me that some of the senior Indian officers complained. I convened a Court of Inquiry, who inspected it and reported that it was indeed adulterated. I happened also to be what was called Cantonment Magistrate, so the offender was brought before me in that office. As I enquired into the case I detected a smirk on the contractor's countenance. He had all along been reckoning on the fact that a second class magistrate could only fine up to fifty rupees, which was far less than the profit he calculated to make by adulterating several thousands of rations. An inspiration came, so I remanded the case.

In my capacity as Chief Signal Officer to the Force, I 'cleared the line' to Army Headquarters in Delhi and requested the Adjutant General to appoint me Provost Marshal. The reply came back with all the speed of electricity. I was a Provost Marshal.

Now this office goes back to the days of King Edward the First, if not earlier. His powers are considerable. Until recently he could hang an offender by the roadside. Possibly these powers still exist; an interesting point for constitutional lawyers to debate. I assumed that they did. The culprit reappeared and was informed that he was to receive two dozen from the cat o' nine tails. The smirk left his face as he was hurried off to the 'triangles', and the cat was taken from the bag for all to see. The atmosphere miraculously changed; truculence faded out, repentence was in the air, and the contractor hastily promised that if the sentence could be suspended, all the adulterated flour would be replaced at his own expense and to the troops' satisfaction. So, justice was tempered with mercy, and all except the delinquent saw the humour of it.

In 1912 I had an assignment to escort up the long mountain road to Chitral a Battalion of the 3rd Gurkhas, who were to relieve another Battalion way up in that far northern principality after their year's tour of duty.

Before we set off on those twenty marches the old 59th Rifles gave a party in honour of one 'Peep' Martin, who was to go with us. Now poor Peep was very large indeed, and an attack of enteric had left him with a vast waist measurement. Perhaps this contributed to his lamented death in Flanders; he was too big for any

26

trench to protect him.

A fellow guest at the party was a civilian Sinologist, who told the company that he believed our Chinese gun might have been made of solid gold. All rushed out to inspect it, but, alas, it was merely of excellent bronze. 'Anyway, let's fire it off.'

So powder was sent for, and portfires. After one or two feeble bangs they greatly increased the charge, whereupon the old gun burst. A large fragment struck Peep in the abdomen, making a big wound there. However, he was not the man to let that keep him back, so along he came with us. Every evening the entire medical talent of the column was mobilized with armfuls of lint and gauze to patch the great gulf. All the rank and file gathered round in their hundreds to admire, applaud and encourage.

Northwards we marched over the great Malakand ridge, soon to be pierced by our enterprising engineers to take the greatest canal tunnel in the world. We passed through the land of Swat, where a war was in progress between the Chief of Dir to one side of our trail, and the up-and-coming Wali of Swat to the other. Both sides, with true Pathan politeness, ceased fire while we passed between them. The Chief of Dir entertained us, not only with his band of pipers, but with discharges from his home-made field gun of 3-inch calibre. His own artificers had made it, a breech-loader with fixed brass cartridges, all made with hand tools. The weak spot, one remembers, lay in the fuses, which could not be depended on to function. But then neither could those made by Woolwich for our Grand Fleet at Jutland. The pipers made up for the lack of detonation from the shells.

So on we marched over the snow of the Lowarai Pass to Chitral and delivered our Gurkhas; then through those half-dozen extremely ferocious Pathan republics, where triggernometry is the only science; and then to the amazing land of Hunza, that remote Moslem principality farthest north in the Emperor's India.

Hunza has no equal in this world. It marches with Russia in the north and with China to the north-east. Its ruler, the Thum is a benevolent autocrat, who, with his people, claims descent from a flanking detachment of the troops of Alexander of Macedon. The lowest part of its main valley is 7,000 feet above sea level, whilst its many mountains run to 25,000 feet and more, bearing some of the world's greatest glaciers outside the polar regions.

The people grow barley from stony fields which a Welsh hill farmer would consider beyond hope; and they do it with small wooden ploughs, whilst the irrigation is from glacier water carried for miles in channels hewn in the face of heaven-reaching rock cliffs. The grain is ground in little wooden water-mills, the only machines in the country. Besides this tillage, the people have sheep, goats and tiny cattle, and in the north are yaks. The health of these people is of course the wonder of dieticians the world over.

All, men and women, wear a stone-coloured ibex tweed of quite surpassing quality enough to turn Harris or Donegal green with envy. The women, often of Macedonian beauty, may be seen ploughing behind their small oxen wearing these long woollen gowns. Politeness and hospitality are the universal rule, so is cheerfulness, and they have the most beautiful manners. There is much dance and song, and, rather surprisingly, wine parties. The wine much resembles sherry. No one has any money at all, but every man has a rifle.

Everyone, rich or poor, plays polo, galloping full split up and down the stony village streets. It is customary to hit the ball in full flight in the air, and not exceptional for a goal to be hit from half way. The hitter gallops with the ball in his left hand which he then throws up to hit with his right, full pitch. It is strange that so few players in these games are ever killed. Stone reefs stick out of the field, everyone 'crosses' at full gallop, and everyone brandishes his stick in every direction. How any quadruped can stand being galloped for three-quarters of an hour on end, at that altitude and on such rocks, boggles the imagination; but they do it.

In 1891 an earlier Thum hurled defiance at the powers to the southward. The consequence was a tiny Indian Army expedition, accompanied by the highly novel Gatling gun. In most gallant fashion they stormed the barrier fort of Nilt, perched, like all the castles in these parts, on a giddily precipitous rock. Immediately the people of Hunza, known as Hunzakuts, buried the hatchet, and in a flash became the most loyal British subjects, most ready to help us against their hated Russian neighbours.

After our short sojourn in Hunza, we returned to Mardan by the Indus route. Peep got to Chitral and back, and his wound healed.

Chapter 6

THE GOLDEN PASSPORT

Providence and the leave roster, neither of which could have heard about Gavrilo Princip, gave me a year's furlough from the spring of 1914.

I had long ached to follow in the footsteps of earlier generations of the Guides, in particular the escort to the grand mission of Sir Thomas Forsyth to Yarkand and Kashgar in 1873; and I yearned to traverse Zungaria, where that famous explorer Colonel Percy Etherton had gone in 1905 on his great journey to the Trans-Siberian homeland of the Moghul emperors as he described it in *Across the Roof of the World*.

The Chinese had regained domination over these vast unmeasured lands nearly a year's journey from Peking, and before any foreigner could travel this new dominion, he had to go through the ancient formalities and apply for a 'Golden Passport' from the Tsung-li-Yamen. The India Office made one apply for this a whole year beforehand, which I did in due and correct form. But after a year it still had not arrived.

We set off anyway and paused in Kashmir for a few days in the peaceful beauty of Srinagar to collect provisions and gear for the long trek ahead, leaving word for the passport to be sent on. We marched from Srinagar on 14 June 1914 and arrived in Leh twelve days later. Here was a little mud rest house where was already bedded down that veteran hunter, Major Cumberland of the Dorsets, who asked if it was my brother he had known at the taking of Kandahar in 1879. This called for tact. Firstly, because it was my father, and secondly, because he had sold a horse to the paternal parent which had not given entire satisfaction. In fact, we heard afterwards that he had called it The Baker, on the principle of 'pull devil, pull baker'. The ancient sportsman was off to the Chang Chen Ho to secure, if he could, a specimen of the very, very rare *Ovis Brookei* for the benefit of the Dorchester Museum.

Before we had arrived, a large Italian expedition under the alpinist Dr Filippo de Filippi had departed, taking with it almost all of the available men and ponies. I managed eventually to secure three men: Karim, an Argoon, who proved most useful, and could translate into Urdu for me; Puntsog, a Tibetan, thoroughly uncivilized, but cheerful and willing; and a Turk named Sidiq. Sidiq turned out to possess neither endurance, pluck nor intelligence, despite the Swedish silver medal he had received serving with Sven Hedin in 1906. I afterwards found that very few inhabitants of Central Asia had escaped becoming the recipients of this decoration.

The main pillar of our little party was my orderly Ghulam Ali, a young Pathan NCO. A job for Ghulam and myself was to collect a dozen of those ponies who needed to be so exceeding tough that they could carry loads along twenty-nine grim marches, where there is not even a hovel or a yard of cultivation, and over all those lung-searing passes. We managed to find ten.

For the next two days we travelled on up the Indus bank, then struck north over the Chang La, that mighty 19,000-footer – a good, tough introduction to the next half-dozen lung-rackers. We camped at 16,500 feet by a lake in a grassy alp. The next day found us at the last human habitation, a veritable world's end called Shaiok, and we left all signs of humanity for many days. Rough marching up the valley of the upper Shaiok lay before us, away from the accustomed caravan trail because my official permission was in return for a promise to make a reconnaissance report for the General Staff.

On the third day we crossed the Chang Chen Ho just where it meets the main river, and gazed up its valley eastwards towards illimitable desert stretches of nothing at all, which would take months to cross. For that matter, to the north in front of us was nothing but rocks, snow and ice, bordered by immense mountains, holding here and there, every few miles, a tiny patch of grass, so scrubby as to be barely discernible. But even these

were valuable in helping the ponies to fill their deserving stomachs. When the evening drew on it was a matter of much anxiety to decide whether to halt and pitch our tiny camp where this vegetation could be seen, or whether to press on so as to gain a few more miles that day, and hope to find another patch. The risks of leaving the ponies without their night's grazing were not small. To stave off famine I used a .22 rifle to stalk pigeons. The food supply for a day often depended on the result of a single shot. I had hoped to find antelope all up the Shaiok, but not a single one of any kind came in sight, though we saw plenty of skeletons and heads.

On the tenth day we found ourselves having to cross a bright red stream where it met a bright yellow one. Here we encountered a man named Ahmed Akhun, who was bringing up supplies for Dr de Filippi, camped on the Dipsang plain, our first main objective. At the next tumbling river Ahmed Akhun told us that two Mecca pilgrims from Yarkand had been drowned there, together with their camel, a couple of days before. We now had to cross this river.

Where the track hit, it was some twenty yards wide and coming down hard. Ghulam Ali and I collected the party on the bank; at which moment up came our cheery Tibetan, Puntsog, much bedraggled with water streaming off his pigtail. He, or rather Karim, translating, explained that he had been swept off his feet in the river we had previously crossed, unnoticed by the rest of us, and carried a long way down on to a handy sandbank, from which he had been rescued.

The obvious solution lay in mounting the two strongest ponies to get ropes across. Luckily our baggage ropes were long enough, so Ahmed Akhun and I just managed to struggle across with them to rocks on the far side. Using a stirrup iron as a runner, the loaded ponies were then hauled across one by one, each with his bridle lashed to the running stirrup. This took several hours, but towards the end, when Ghulam Ali was bringing up the rear, the stirrup leather became unbuckled and he too was swept down into the roaring waters. Good luck stepped in, and we rescued him, jammed between a pinnacle of rock and the foot of the cliff.

A little further on there was another crossing of the same kind, which proved no easier. Sidiq's courage began to desert him, and he announced that he was 'not for crossing any more rivers'. I had to point out to him that if he did not cross the river he would have no choice but to spend the rest of his life on the little heap of boulders where we then were. So he consented to be hauled across. We repeated the whole procedure, which took quite another two hours, everything getting thoroughly wet by being hauled under water. Of course, when all the loads were over, the ropes remained with the far end tied to the opposite bank. As we could not spare them I had myself lowered down the rope into the water. On the far bank I unhooked them and, placed the loops over one shoulder, and was hauled by brute force across the stream again, mostly under water. The force of the river was so great that it took four men on the rope to make any progress to pull me back through the rushing torrent.

Eight hours march from here our track met that commonly used by the hardy Yarkand caravan men, who come up over the Nubra glacier. The grim character of these men's lives and deaths made itself directly clear to us, as for many marches northwards from here the trail is bordered by two banks of bleached bones, and beyond them on all sides only rock, ice, snow and sky.

The valley floor now rose to 17,000 feet, and it took a big hillside to look down on it. However, mountains here run big, and looming above us, away to our left, was K2, the eastern buttress of what is perhaps the greatest mountain wall in the world.

Up to this point we had been guided by a very old map made by one of those wonderful and dauntless pioneers of the Survey of India, Colonel Thomas Montgomerie. He would have called it a reconnaissance map, but it was amazingly true to the country. In his day contours had not really been invented, but the hachuring, beautifully engraved on a copper plate, still makes me wonder and admire as I look at it ninety years after it was made. This map led us up to the wide, lofty Dipsang plain and to Dr de Filippi's highly civilized base camp, where we were most hospitably welcomed by the Marquess Ginori and Professor Alessandri. The doctor himself was up on the Remo glacier. One of the Marquess' meteorological sounding-balloons had descended into a remote part of Tibet. A special commission, strong in astrologers, was sent from Lhasa to examine it. They foretold great events. Little did they know.

We camped at 17,900 feet by good water, truly on the roof of the world. Poor Ghulam had a touch of mountain sickness. Providence, however, caused an antelope to fall to my rifle, so famine recoiled from us for a few days.

The next day we topped the great Karakorum itself at some 18,600 feet, and here the old map seemed to go wrong. The Chinese claimed this to be their frontier, but nowhere could we see any sign of it. The only thing we found was a cairn marking where Dad Mahommed had murdered the explorer George Whitaker Hayward in 1885, and was hunted down seven years later by Lieutenant Hamilton Bower over these mighty hills, and finally handed over to the executioner's axe in Yarkand.

Two days more took us to the easy Suget pass of 17,600, and the way at last began to march down hill, to the little Chinese mud fortalice of Suget, with the imposing range of the Karanghu Tagh for a backcloth. Now we felt we were back again in the world of men, from those almost lunar landscapes behind us. We pitched our tiny tents near a patch of barley on the enchanting green grass.

Soon enough a polite young Chinese official, named Ssu Yeh, came out from the frontier post to greet us. The revolution must have passed him by, because he still wore a long blue silk habit and immense finger nails. For twenty-seven Indian rupees he provided us with 420lbs of barley, and as much flour as we needed. Then, with much diffidence, he explained that orders were orders and he was forced to ask even a welcome visitor like myself for his passport.

When I say asked, he put his request in Chinese to a Kirghiz, who translated it into Turkish to my Karim, who then passed it on to me in Urdu. Happily all this gave me time to reflect, and so to deal with the problem of not having that passport. Immediate action, as the machine-gunners say, was to dig out a bottle of cherry brandy, carried along for just such a crisis. This, from an enamelled pint jug, was not unwelcome. The cherry brandy I supplemented by a fair amount of small talk, itself expanded by the triple-banked interpreting. No doubt the sporting instincts of the Kirghiz and caravan men were excited by hopes of seeing how I was going to outflank officialdom. The cherry brandy in time showed excellent results on the diplomatic front, so then out came a bottle of crème de menthe and another mug, which brought about a still broader outlook.

When this had soaked in I extracted from my papers the wrapping of a package of Keating's powder. In those days this bore Mr Keating's instructions in the scripts of some sixteen oriental languages. Better still, it had at its head representations in real gold of the dozen or so medals he had been awarded, at Chicago, the Exposition Universelle in Paris, and so forth. Between a hiccup or two, little Ssu Yeh admitted that he had never seen a passport quite up to this level. Another swig of cherry brandy, and out came his little brush and his stick of Chinese ink, with which he put quite the best form of visa on to the Keating document. A few final tots, and then off he zigzagged to his *Beau Geste* stronghold and to tomorrow's hangover.

We much hoped that he would appease his superiors in Peking. It transpired that in Imperial days an official, even in distant Turkestan or Tibet, a year's journey away, might, if he offended, receive a rescript instructing him to get himself decapitated under local arrangements. Such orders were never disobeyed. I hated to think of that polite little man's head rolling in the sawdust.

We moved on quickly the next day, accompanied by the Kirghiz headman who came with us with four of his Bactrian camels to help us over the deep, swift rivers ahead, which were too much for our laden ponies. The most serious of the rivers was the Togra Su, coming down with great force and quite impassable. At the 'ford', we met a merchant, camped there with his caravan, who explained that he had been waiting a fortnight to cross. As the Togra Su was glacier fed, I hoped that the water would subside in the morning, which it did. The fording had to be done diagonally across a couple of islands, the camels carrying the baggage. All had considerable difficulty in keeping their footing against the force of the current, and the only Kashmiri pony I had, straying a little away from the proper ford, was swept away in a flash. After a few minutes his nose appeared some 300 yards downstream amidst the seething waters, and that was the last we saw of him. Another pony foolishly followed him, but was not sucked quite so far into the torrent, and just managed to scramble ashore lower down.

We camped on the last of the 17,000-foot passes, called locally

Grim Darwan meaning Barley Pass, only there was none.

We started early in the morning, through heavy snow, and up a very steep gully. A heavy climb of two hours took us to the summit, a knife edge. The snow suddenly stopped, and we got a magnificent view of the unknown mountains to the east. A correspondingly steep descent took us to an open, grassy Pamir and undulations where marmots abounded. Here was a large encampment of Kirghiz who brought us an excellent supply of curds, and also some magnificent butter in a lordly dish, which was very welcome after the weeks we had spent without it. The kind Beg was a man of over seventy with a long grey beard. He remembered Forsyth's Mission of 1873 with its escort of Guides cavalry, in whose footsteps we were following.

One more pass, a trifle of 14,500 feet, and we came to more level going, marching from oasis to oasis, little green paradises in the surrounding desert, their gardens and verdant beauty watered by little bubbling rills.

The hospitality of the people was breathtaking. At every halt many great trays would be spread out for us on rugs, piled with melons of numberless species, and grapes, pears and peaches, incredibly huge. The oasis of Karghalik was reached the next day.

From here onwards, on every march, all British subjects, whether Hindu or Mohammedan, would come out many miles to meet us, on their best horses and dressed in their best clothes. They all seemed extremely pleased to see a British officer, and did everything they could to make us comfortable. There were a considerable number of Afghans, who had no hesitation in telling me that they were British subjects, and were extremely pleased to hear that I came from Mardan and could speak Pushtu.

The next two days took us to Yarkand. I tried travelling in a *mapa*, a Chinese cart with huge wheels and tyres studded with gigantic nails. The vibration caused by these was beyond belief, though by sitting on an air cushion I managed to endure for a few hours at a time.

In Yarkand there was a British Trade Agent, an Afghan, who went by the title of 'White Beard'. He spared no pains to do everything for me, providing a sumptuously carpeted room in his sarai, vast quantities of fruit, tea and sweets, and even some Chinese visiting cards ready painted on vermillion paper, ready for my call on the Amban and his Yamen. We sent on my cards half an hour ahead, and then White Beard and the five of us, on the best horses, rode up to the gates of the Yamen.

The drill took us through seven gates in succession, and then we dismounted to meet the Amban. He wore a black uniform of European cut with a dragon-crested cap. We conversed through double relays of interpreters, because it was not etiquette for a Chinese official to speak Turkish. The tea was taken with full ceremonial, and he sent me a present of grain, grass and fuel. I countered with a much-appreciated bottle of crème de menthe.

Chapter 7

A BUFF SLIP

In the third week of August 1914 we found ourselves marching, just after midnight, out of Yarkand straight towards the North Star under the spell of the great desert of Takla Makan, on a trail many, many centuries old, along which silk was brought to the emperors of Rome, the silk worms smuggled in hollow canes. Sometimes my Pathan henchman and I marched or trotted over the hard track of the gravel plain, and sometimes we floundered through the soft sands of the dunes.

In the morning, before the first dawn, our little caravan settled down to sleep on the plastered earthen shelves that served for beds in Turkestan. Waking up in full daylight we were surprised to find ourselves sharing the encampment with a patrol of the 4th Orenburg Cossacks under a subaltern called Chemaiev, a famous name in Russian imperial expansion. We breakfasted together with his half-dozen troopers and in French learnt a vague rumour of an impending war apparently between Russia and Germany; but no mention of France or of Britain.

Chemaiev assumed that we should be unsympathetic to Germany. He also assumed that Italy would be an enemy, and wondered whether it were not his duty to round up the members of de Filippi's expedition when they should come down off the Karakoram.

That could not take place for many days, so we agreed that we must both push on to Kashgar and there find out what was really happening in distant Europe.

At Kashgar we stayed with the Consul General Sir George Macartney and his charming wife, who had held the fort for the

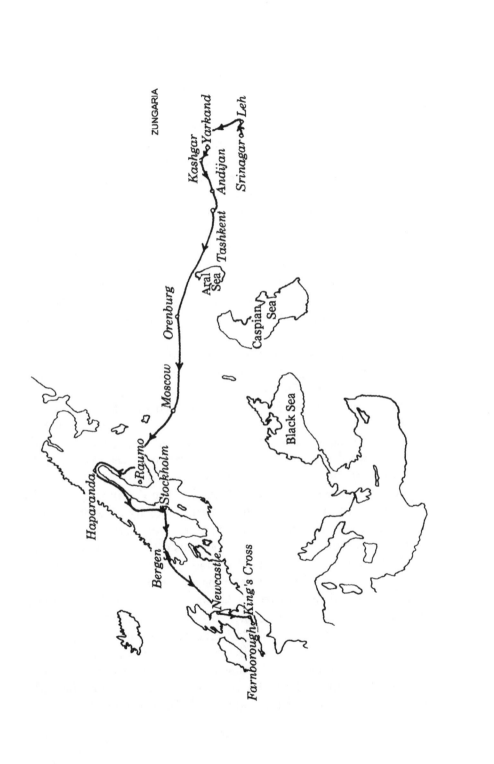

British and Indian Governments, staving off every sort of Russian aggression for over twenty years.

When at last the Kirghiz postman came galloping in from Russia over those sixteen marches from Andijan, his leather saddle bags bulging with news from Europe, we knew then that the Cossacks were our allies. Now no doubt remained that King George was at war with his German cousin. We had reports of a naval fight in the North Sea, of a British Army on its way to Flanders, the retreat from Mons, and the siege of Königsberg.

This news decided my future movements; so my long-planned journey to Zungaria came to a sudden end. We decided that Ghulam Ali should go back to the Regiment, so, giving him a horse, a bag of flour and some cash, Sir George and I indicated the general direction of the British Empire, and off he set, over the Chinese Pamirs and through the strange lands of Hunza and Gilgit, forty or fifty days' march away. I little guessed that the next time I should see him would be on a blood-clotted stretcher in the salient of Ypres.

Cossack hospitality is something quite remarkable, and the farewell party which they threw for their solitary British ally lacked for nothing. The sun was up before it ended.

The sleeping-off process was compressed to a few hours, and then I and three men of the Guides, including Havildar Awal Nur, who was to accompany me on many adventures, began a long hot ride westward towards Russia. Our initial goal was Andijan, the terminus of the Russian railway, with a couple of 15,000 feet passes in between. After the Chang La, the Karakoram and the Grim Darwan one felt these to be hardly worthy of notice. If one got a trifle out of breath on the way up, this seemed a cause for shame; although the number of skeletons scattered about testified to the trouble other caravans had had crossing in bad weather.

A dozen marches brought us to the ancient and entirely Moslem town of Osh whence a cart road runs to Andijan and the railway. So after many bone-aching days in the racking saddles of central Asia we hired an *izdvoschik*. Its velocity, after our pack caravans, seemed terrific, and we hardly seemed to have regained breath when we descended to a European-style hotel with knives, forks and all that sort of thing. There were even sheets upon the beds, but the basins were of that odd quasi-Turko-Persian type which trickle water from above on to one's hands and acrobatically upturned features.

I had frequently heard Tashkent called the Paris of Central Asia, and it was certainly a remarkable city. The cantonment was absolutely European to look at, with hotels, shops and banks, electric trams and wide Boulevards, quite startling to the eyes of one still mesmerized by the glaciers, soaring peaks and deserts so recently traversed.

But there was no time for sightseeing. King George was unmistakably at war with Germany. I needed a pass to travel across Russia, so applied to the Governor-General's office, which produced not only a pass, but a berth in a special express which was to take the badly-needed machine-gunners of the 3rd Turkestan Rifle Regiment to the Galician front. All payment was declined, so for very shame one had to contribute the price of the tickets to the Russian Red Cross.

Fifteen days and fifteen nights we spent on the train. Every dozen miles we passed sidings crammed with other troop trains full of Turkestan and Siberian regiments moving to the Western Front, a symbol of that rapid mobilization, and the smooth, hitchless working of the Imperial Russian railways which was such a surprise to the planners of the Great General Staff.

Conspicuous on their flat trucks were seemingly innumerable modern field guns, a sharp and bitter contrast to India's penury in such weapons. In 1914 and 1915 the only field gun in Europe or Asia which had no high explosive shell was the British, a lack which was destined to cost our infantry very dear indeed. In the Army of India artillery deficiency was beyond belief.

The journey over the immensities of Kazakistan left indelible pictures. The line was single, with passing places every score of versts, where a steel tower gave us water. We stretched our legs, drank tea with lemon slices from vast samovars, and gazed before and behind at the endless parallels of steel, stretching to a pinpoint on either horizon over the curves of the planet. As the coasts of the Aral Sea approached, the deserts became steppes or prairies flaming with great patches of brilliant wild flowers. It was strange then to see a lighthouse and fishing vessels in the middle of a huge continent.

The Russian machine-gunners, whose train we shared, took

41

their British ally to their collective bosom. This machine-gun company – or more particularly their weapons – opened one's eyes. The guns were light Maxims, not quite so light as our later Vickers but with steel, not bronze, water jackets. The locks seemed to be the original way up and not inverted, from which one might deduce that the Russian Army anticipated the British in adopting a lighter gun. The British Army in Flanders did not achieve such machine-gun companies until nearly two years later.

Very early in the morning, the day after we left the sea coast behind, we clattered over the bridge into Europe and to a transcendentally beautiful sight, the 'rosy fingered dawn' striking on the domes of Orenburg. The rays reflected themselves back from those bronze tulip roofs, making delicate colour pictures on their patina of turquoise and cerulean.

In Europe the steppes and prairies of Cossack and Kazak gave way gradually to ploughed fields and the cottages of Christian peasants. At the junction of the railway from Siberia, we parted from the friendly machine-gun company, who headed for the Galician front, while we moved on to Moscow.

We spent two days in Moscow. Japanese 11-inch howitzers trundled through the streets on their way towards Königsberg to fight on the side of their late enemies. I shaved off my portentous beard of many weeks' growth, and travelled on to Petersburg, as it was then, where a picture remains of the distinctive strawberry-coloured livery of the Imperial household, whom one saw driving about the streets on errands.

Our Military Attaché there handed us an envelope for Whitehall, highly secret as usual, coupled with a warning not to get interned in neutral Sweden. Off we went to Rauma, but an enemy cruiser prevented our crossing the Gulf of Bosnia. So we chuffed up, in a fourth-class carriage – there was no fifth – to wooden-built Haparanda in the extreme north where Finland meets Sweden, then back down on the long train journey south to Stockholm; from that beautiful capital to Bergen, and so across the already mine-strewn North Sea to Newcastle, and King's Cross.

I now had time to wonder what officialdom would say or do to me. I had already been in trouble over the affair in the Ambela Pass (Chapter 5), when the Civil Power clamoured for my blood but the military High Command fortunately handed out a commendation.

Then there was the awkward business of that 'Golden' Chinese passport, or rather the absence of it. The Foreign Office had bungled, but officialdom being what it is, there was every reason to expect that a black mark would be scored up against a junior officer who could not answer back.

And there was a third abyss into which a fall was possible. An extreme type of pipeclay-minded Adjutant General might easily have told himself that I should have marched south from Kashgar with Ghulam Ali back to the Orderly Room of our 1st Battalion. But some atavistic, if non-regulation, instinct had told me that the way to confront Germans and to the sound of the guns lay to the north-west.

In the War Office, I was genially received with my documents by the Director of Military Intelligence, who was glad to hear my news about our Russian ally.

By a fluke I found Bertie Reynolds, he whose Bristol biplane had turned upside down on the way to those 1911 manoeuvres, stuck in the War Office with a broken ankle. He said to me, 'Go down to Farnborough and tell them I told you.' He was referring to the remains of the Royal Flying Corps in Great Britain.

He let me know that the Indian Government, in contradistinction to the stalwart peasantry of the Punjab, seemed less than lukewarm about fighting the Germans. They were, in fact, packing those of their officers on leave in England back to Bombay in shoals, aboard the *Dongola*. So ardently did the India Office function on this that even Major Generals queued up for bathrooms on that vessel.

More of that atavistic instinct told me to steer entirely clear of the India Office and go to Farnborough instead, equipped with a 'buff slip' from Bertie. The old Army used to say that many a kind heart beats behind a buff slip.

Chapter 8

TUMULT IN THE AIR

The night was spent on the floor of the Reserve Squadron's office with other pilots, amongst them L.W.B. Rees from West Africa, who was soon to acquire the Victoria Cross and survive.

Next morning I found myself the senior officer of all His Majesty's military aircraft in Great Britain, and so took over the confidential safe. It contained two left boots.

A handful of damaged BE2as and Longhorn Maurice Farmans were being patched up by the few other ranks, so it seemed one ought to try to fly them somehow, regardless of whether one really knew how to. Some fellow had finished mending a BE2a. She was a pleasant-looking aircraft, and I took her up over Aldershot's Laffan's Plain and Caesar's Camp. I found she was quite ready to turn round to the left; on attempting to turn to the right, however, all seemed to go wrong. In those days a 'spin' was a certain prelude to a coroner's inquest, so, making valour give way to discretion, I turned to the left at an enormous radius and, by the interposition of Providence, reached the ground. An inspection revealed that the riggers had fixed a BE2b wing on one side of the machine, and a BE2a wing on the other.

Before long, orders came through for us to do something about the Kaiser's airships. It would have to be done at night. Luckily a pilot with experience of night flying came to hand, one A.C. Cooper, and I became his observer-gunner.

My duty was the management of a really fearsome engine of war known as the 'fiery grapnel'. It consisted of a steel tube nearly five feet long filled with TNT. At one end of this tube were four arms with barbed hooks sharpened to razor edges. Outside it was

44

lashed a portentous piece of pyrotechnics like a roman candle with a friction lighter. This awesome contraption was slung between the wheels of the poor little BE, which weighed less than 600lbs all up. To one end of it was shackled a couple of thousand feet of steel cable, which was wound on a drum located between the observer-gunner's knees. There was also a rope to pull, with which to ignite the friction lighter and detonate the bomb.

The great idea was that the BE, having first found an airship, should climb to about 1,000 feet above her, then steer an intercepting course, releasing the fiery grapnel shortly before the vital meeting. This pulled the lanyard igniting the great firework, and the whole should then run out to the length of its 1,000 feet or so of cable, burning briskly. The pilot would then hook the sharp flukes of the grapnel into any suitable part of the airship. At that moment the observer-gunner, if he was not now mesmerized with fright, was to cut the cable with a pair of pliers (supplied by the management). With any luck, the roman candle would then burn down to the detonator of the TNT, which would blow the airship in half, while our little aeroplane might flap away unharmed.

This procedure, however, never came off, mainly because no BE could climb high enough to get above an airship steered by a normally vigilant airship captain, who could, of course, every now and then stop his engines and listen for those of the enemy.

We also had primitive 20-pound bombs, but the results were not encouraging. After one hectic night turnout without finding the enemy, we landed. I examined our bomb load and found them stowed in rough deal boxes, nailed to the lower fuselage with carpenters' ten-penny nails which had been driven right through everything. When I reproached the sergeant rigger concerned for this somewhat barbaric piece of work, he told me that the job had been done in a hurry by the cook's mate.

Another of our pilots took off with the bombs on a foggy night. He cruised about optimistically until his amazed eyes saw a great grey shape looming in the murk just below him. His hand was on the release, but just at that moment he suddenly realized that the great grey mass was the Farnborough airship shed.

By this time we were all impatient to get to France, myself especially because of the stories reaching me of the horrors being suffered by my brother officers of the Guides and my dedicated jawans in the trenches of Flanders and Artois. But our passing out was delayed by sundry crashes, brought about in part no doubt by this same impatience and tension.

I had the misfortune to crash a renovated Farman Longhorn, which I was testing, virtually in the presence of the great 'Boom' Trenchard himself, who sent me off to the Central Flying School, Upavon, for further training.

There, one of my teachers invited me to receive a lesson on how to fly a weird product of the department which we called the 'Bloater' – not of course its official name. We took off reasonably, and at a couple of thousand feet he shouted to me to take over the dual control (there were no voice pipes then).

'Have you got her?' yelled my teacher.

'Yes,' I replied, 'but you know I have never flown one of these things before.'

To which he replied, 'Neither have I, old boy.'

However, Salisbury Plain is pretty large and we managed to land. In due course I received a parchment certificate, and headed for France.

To the airmen of those days France was another world. That enlightened land was his spiritual home, partly because of the pioneer Captain Ader and his bat-winged, steam-powered Avion, and partly because, more prosaically, there were no hedges, the English flying man's nightmare. The frequent forced-landing fatalities of English flying in those days were nearly always due to the deadly hedge. So we blessed the French farmer, wondering also, as we do to this day, how it is that French cows can be humbugged into wearing head-collars whilst the Anglo-Saxon cannot.

Our Flight shook down first under Stuffy Dowding at St Omer, headquarters of Sir John French. A never-to-be forgotten sight was of an entire cavalry corps, still in their cuirasses and those wide garance pantaloons, who marched eastwards past our aerodrome to be used as infantry in the French trenches. The blood baths of December 1914 had passed by and the infantry began to wonder if their horror was over; but much more was to come.

We had a few relatively fast French Morane and Nieuports, and a good Bristol single-seater or two. For these aircraft, the butcher's bill was due more to flying accidents than to the enemy's fire. This was not so for our older and slower types, such as the Shorthorn Farman. At 4,000 feet or so these had an airspeed of barely 40 mph; on most days the wind came from the south-west and seldom with a velocity of less than 30 mph. So one's homeward speed over the ground was hardly that of a cantering horse, and well within the capacity of Jerry's painfully numerous 77-mm anti-aircraft guns. They had plenty of practice, and were rapidly becoming unpleasantly accurate.

Our own anti-aircraft weapons were rather pathetic 13-pounders taken from the Horse Artillery. Shrapnel was their only missile. However, RFC coteries were then full of the yarn about their famous Gordon Bell, pioneer of pioneers. He was not a 'regular' in any sense, but an outstanding Bristol Scout pilot. As he flew back from a patrol his course took him just over Ploegsteert Wood. One of these British anti-aircraft sections lay in wait behind its western edge. Its commander was a coast gunner Captain who apparently had been told to shoot at everything he saw. As ill luck would have it, a single fluky shot from his 13-pounder knocked one plug out of Gordon Bell's Gnome engine with a single lone shrapnel ball. Even this amazing engine could not run with one plug out, and Gordon Bell was forced to glide into friendly territory, which he was just, only just, able to reach. He wrapped his little aircraft around the top of a tree, detached himself from the cockpit, and proceeded to climb down the trunk. Now it happened that an Artillery General had picked that very moment to inspect, and it had not dawned upon either this general or his captain that the aeroplane they had been shooting at was British. They sprang into their car, waded across a field next to the wood, and were most surprised to see a British aeroplane perched in the tree top. Still unaware of the facts the General reached the foot of the tree just as did Gordon Bell, only from a different direction.

'Have you had an accident, my boy?' asked the General.

'N-no, you old f-fool,' replied our airman, who stuttered badly and was fully aware of who had shot him down, 'I always l-land like this.'

In proper brass-hat fury the General roared, 'Who are you?

What's your name, and what is your number?'

So our Gordon, even more wrathful, replied, 'If you w-want to kn-know my n-number, you had b-better shin up the t-tree and get it off my t-t-tail.'

Still blind with rage, the General ordered him into arrest. Just then the artillery captain suddenly grasped the situation, but too late. The General tried in vain to retract his order, but Gordon Bell insisted on his right to remain in close arrest whilst the scandal was reported to GHQ.

Much oil had to be poured out on the troubled waters that raged between the Royal Artillery and the Royal Flying Corps. There was no court martial.

One thing we did have at that early time was some really quite excellent Vickers 'Gun-Buses'. Their Monosoupape engines did not always run, but when they did they pushed those two-seaters along quite fast. The pilot and gunner sat in front of everything; so their field of fire was excellent, and, to crown all, they had guns. Colonel Lewis's admirable machine gun was just beginning to seep into the RFC, despite the obstruction of our technical 'experts'. It was Sefton-Brancker we had to thank, and his genius for cutting red tape. He was born to be a smuggler, and we junior officers never really found out how he managed to outwit officialdom. The upshot was that red tape was baffled, and the German *Fliegers,* who at that moment had no ahead-shooting machines, became justly scared of the Vickers Gun-Bus; nor could they distinguish our other pusher biplanes from the Vickers, and so steered rapidly away from us. As a result, in those days we felt very much on top of the German in the air, and prayed only to meet one suddenly round the corner of a cloud with no time to get away. In the late autumn when the enemy acquired the services of Anthony Fokker and his novel weapon, the boot was very much on the other foot.

Our main work lay in finding targets for our heavier artillery, such as it was, and directing the fire of its guns on to those targets. This involved flying firstly downwind over where we expected to find German positions, such as a row of gun pits. Then one turned painfully back into the wind and signalled on our primitive wireless the target's position on the map. 'Primitive' is the right word, because we had tiny, battery-powered transmitters only, of the spark type. There were no valves, and the artillery and a couple of our own men, rather wonderfully, received our signals on a crystal and a cat's whisker.

Almost daily our patrol work took us over in this way, and into the path of the Kaiser's Flak artillery with its rapidly growing skill.

Our feeble engines could barely achieve 5,000 feet, so often we drifted into small-arms fire. Somewhere about this level the Mauser bullet reached the top of its trajectory, and so when the machine guns were firing I saw their bullets turning over in the air and glinting in the sun, like shoals of whitebait pretending to be salmon leaping. Their velocity was then reduced, but quite enough to split a propeller, or a tail boom, or to cut a control. The enemy continued to get more shooting practise at our expense, whilst our air mechanics, as they were then called, got more and more practice at patching holes with fabric and Titanine dope.

In February, shortly after coming out, I had to 'range' a battery of 60-pounders. The day was very windy from the south-west, i.e. from France towards Germany, and the clouds were very low (about 3,800 to 4,000 feet), i.e. within rifle range, but I decided to go over the German lines and risk it. We were heavily shelled for a few minutes (accurately) and received several hits from shrapnel and high explosive. Having examined the first target and decided that it contained no Germans, I directed Spence, the pilot, over the second target and signalled to the guns to fire. We were then heavily shelled by the Germans for some time receiving a good many hits. I saw then that the two lower tail booms were splintered by shells and decided to go home, as the machine might have crumpled up. On turning homewards we were very nearly kept stationary by the strong south-westerly wind, and so presented an easy target which the Germans took full advantage of. Spence was hit on the sleeve and I in the foot by splinters. We then climbed into a cloud to escape the shells, but lost headway and still got shelled. So we descended again and, losing height to gain speed, crossed the trenches at about 1,700 feet, receiving a good many hits from machine-gun and rifle fire; one of these hit a connecting rod in the engine and stopped it dead, with a loud crash. Spence landed very skilfully about 1,100 yards inside our trenches. The machine was then shelled by the Germans and destroyed.

A month later, at the battle of St Eloi, my task was again to cooperate with a battery of 60-pounders in action near Nieppe, not far from Armentières, in order to silence an enemy heavy battery which menaced our infantry.

We took off and climbed to 4,500 feet, and called up the gunners, who responded smartly, spreading canvas strips on the ground to show that their guns were loaded and layed. Then over the target we made the signal letter G in Morse, which told the artillery to fire. I turned laboriously upwind whilst our shell sailed slowly towards the Germans. I saw it burst in a cloud of black smoke.

Before long, numerous white triangles appeared in the upper surfaces of the wings. These white excrescences quickly became more and more crowded on the fabric; and, looking back, I was surprised to see that our nice white tail had turned black. It took a few moments to realize that this was because our engine oil had betaken itself from its proper place in the sump to a most improper one on the rudders and elevators. Still a few moments later, strange noises emanated from our poor little 80-horse motor and then our aftermost piston on the port side appeared, in the stark light of the morning, to have disembarrassed itself of its confining cylinder. The engine, understandably, ceased to perform its task of keeping us in the air. A tail-boom was also severed at that moment, so we glided down towards a field near Ploegsteert Wood, wondering what was to become of us.

As we rapidly descended every German for a considerable distance around us discharged what piece he had at us. I felt a huge blow on my seat and remarked silently, 'Thank heavens for that steel plate just issued to us!'

Soon we were a few feet over our own infantry trenches and breathed again as the plane just took us over a small fold in the ground which hid us from the German riflemen and their multitudinous machine-gunners.

We landed close behind our own line, and walked round to assess the damage, wondering how the Farman could have flown in that condition. Then a genuine 'Old Bill' British infantryman of the 1914 winter strolled over to us. He wore a stocking cap, his muddy greatcoat cut short about his buttocks, gumboots stuffed with straw, and old socks were drawn over the muzzle and bolt of his rifle. He remarked jealously, '*We* never get a chance to shoot at a bloody aeroplane.'

I lifted the seat cushion, expecting to find a dent in the steel plate. It was not there. Someone had blundered; but a nice shiny Mauser bullet lay embedded in the woodwork, a small fraction of an inch short of full penetration. Hence that mighty wallop. Indeed, a bullet always deals one a blow far heavier than one would expect.

The efficient German knew exactly where the wreckage lay, and as air mechanics Doolittle and Prance struggled with the pliers, a steady rain of field howitzer shells came dropping all about. The machine was flown away early the next morning, and the mechanics were awarded the Distinguished Conduct Medal.

On the first day of the battle of Neuve Chapelle, our flight force landed just behind the village, and as we went up to extricate it, we passed, in the dusk, a column of Garwhal infantry, moving up to their position on the left of the Indian attack, in which they were destined to gain much fame. We wondered how many of those marching would be alive by the next evening.

We heard our orders read over. Our Flight was to report the movement forward of any German reinforcements, to pick out enemy batteries firing against us, and to put our own batteries on to their targets. Particularly, if we saw our own shells falling away from a target, we were to correct.

Our only clue to where our shells came from was to be the colour of their smoke. The ancient, 6-inch howitzers were filled with Lyddite, and gave off a vile, yellow smoke, because their fuses were inefficient and did not detonate the picric acid sufficiently. The few shells from the 9.2s were TNT-filled, and gave good big black bursts, like the much smaller bursts of the 60-pounders. The 4.7 shells of the Haldanian territorial batteries were filled with black powder of the eighteenth century sort, and so threw up white bursts. However, these guns were worn out, their driving bands seldom held their eroded rifling, and so their fire was hardly worth troubling with, from the point of view of the other side.

Spence and I went up at about half-past eight in the clear morning, just before our artillery bombardment sprang an excellent surprise on the Germans. At about 4,500 feet we went in, with a fair wind behind us, eastwards towards the villages on Aubers slope.

If the enemy infantry were taken by surprise, his anti-aircraft gunners certainly were not. At Orgies was a most efficient battery. We had time to see that no infantry were marching on the roads, when the enemy's shell bursts started really pounding our poor Maurice Farman. One soon lost count of the hits. One shrapnel bullet went into the petrol tank. This had no immediate effect, but after we had gone some miles into 'Germany' the engine stopped.

The only remedy was to turn westwards again, towards home, and try to glide those painful miles back. We came over the Bois de Biez, already devastated by shells but still with plenty of undergrowth. There was a very vivid horror of becoming a prisoner, and we hoped to hide in that brushwood until our infantry came through.

Suddenly, as if by magic, the engine started itself; then it stopped again. Three times did this maddening machine perform thus; but at last it stopped for good. All the time, more and more bullets and shell fragments were coming up from the ground, in vast numbers. So many bullets were coming that I felt I really must keep my hands inside the linen covering of the nacelle, foolishly obsessed with an instinct for self-preservation.

On our right, down in the enemy's wide trench, were densely-packed masses of German, probably Westphalian, infantry, roughly four-deep. They still wore their flat caps, banded with crimson, and we were near enough to note their china-blue eyes, which made me think they were Bavarians.

We passed about 500 feet over the enemy trench, and, in fact, through the white smoke of our own shrapnel, evoking a roar of musketry which filled the machine full of holes. A minute later we were on the ground, making a passable landing under the cir-cumstances. Collecting our somewhat scattered wits, we saw a unit of our Horse Artillery in action, with its battery headquarters not far distant, in a cottage, to which we took refuge.

The commander telephoned to La Corgue, to tell our squadron that it now had one less aeroplane than it had at breakfast time. Then there entered a bombardier, saying, 'There's an aeroplane down in the next field. Looks like ours.' So off we went to see.

The field was enormous, very muddy, and suffused with leaden missiles. These all missed us, and we reached a metalled road, by which one of our own flight's BE2s was almost buried in a grim catastrophe. The engine was well into the ground, pilot and observer were dead and mangled, and hardly a stick remained unbroken. It seemed as though she had been hit directly, by a howitzer shell well up on its trajectory. Soon enough an ambulance appeared and we could look around. Nothing of the aeroplane was worth saving, except the compass.

Meanwhile, we found that our aeroplane had 300 holes in it, a Western Front record. Of these, no less than 70 were in the tail assembly, and these were all fair, round bullet holes from rifle and machine guns. The rest, in the main place, were from ragged shell-fragments. This was most instructive because it showed that enemy infantry, like beginners shooting pheasants, always aimed too far back.

When the engine was stripped down, we found that a handful of jagged, needle-like slivers of steel had fallen into the conical funnel at the bottom of the petrol tank. These stopped the flow of petrol, but not completely. After a minute or so, a carburettor-full of petrol was able to seep through. The propeller was wind-milling, and this accounted for those three amazing stops and starts.

A most cogent lesson of this, and other long, seemingly hopeless glides, was that of what one may call '*Anaesthesia Livingstoneia*'. When that explorer was carried away in the jaws of a lion, he records that he felt nothing and maintained only a detached interest in the proceedings. As we came downwards that morning, the same feeling that one was not really concerned came over one. Vision became very acute, but the principal character seemed to be someone else.

Next day, the battle went on. We were briefed the night before, by Stuffy. We were actually allotted a very few rounds from the Coventry ordnance works' excellent 15-inch howitzers. The task became difficult, because a haze came over to mask the battlefield. Our target was Aubers village itself, on the top of the ridge. The early afternoon was still sunny above the haze, and as we flew towards Aubers village, our little aeroplane was shaken until it nearly turned over. At the same moment, we saw a vivid flash of burnished copper, bright in the sun. This was the driving-band of one of our own 15-inch shells, on its slow journey towards Aubers, which had only just missed us; hence the violent shock of the air-wave. That shell did not explode, but, although the haze grew denser, we continued to fire off another, making the signal as we flew downwind over the village.

As we turned, for a moment I lost sight of the houses. The mist had thickened, even at that moment. As I gazed, we came vertically over, so that the layer of mist became thinner: I could see better, and, to my astonished eyes, it seemed as if a dark, pine forest had suddenly grown up where the village was.

For some moments I was bewildered, until I realized that this was a most excellent detonation of that great, bursting charge of TNT, right on the village itself. We heard afterwards that a reinforcing battalion had been in the process of falling-in on the village street, and had derived the full benefit of our shell.

Much longer afterwards, we found that a certain Slavonic lance corporal, had found himself at the time at a regimental headquarters at Aubers. His name was Adolf Schickelgruber. I imagine that our shot must have missed him by at most a few hundred yards.

Chapter 9

WITH THE INDIAN ARMY IN FLANDERS

These things happened during the Battle of Neuve Chapelle. Many people in England do not realize what a victory this was, certainly one creditable in proportion to the ammunition expended and to the casualties, cruel as they were. We had taken a fair amount of ground and hundreds of prisoners, more than ever before. Except for the two regiments of Green Jackets in the 8th Division, the success was mainly due to our Indian jawans, who naturally did not write home to England. So, even today, false lessons are drawn. However, a captured German letter was circulated to us. The writer said, 'God knows what the English have put into those brown devils'.

The victory made me very happy, but plunged me into a severe mental struggle. On the one hand, I had committed myself to the Air Arm, which held prospects of a professional future in a new sphere. But at this moment the Royal Flying Corps showed signs of a technical stagnation. Whitehall bureaucracy had harmed it more than could the Kaiser's *Fliegers*. Indeed almost within weeks, the Royal Flying Corps was destined to be pushed almost out of the air by the products of the brain of Anthony Fokker. In April 1915, this was, in truth, only a nightmare of the future, but still one had the grim feeling that what one could do in those obsolete aeroplanes was but a very little contribution to the war itself.

On the other hand, of the eight pre-war companies of the Guides Infantry, no less than five had come to France to replace the terrible losses of the 57th Wilde's Rifles. These five companies comprised men with whom I had served for years and grown to respect. Indeed, I had been conquered and enslaved by their engaging manners and traditions. Patrols and sorties over the German lines were certainly not safe occupations, but at least the airman spent his nights under cover, in a bed, and in pyjamas. The infantryman lived in a purgatory of shells and mortar bombs to which he had almost no reply, and which slaughtered its dedicated battalions as never before in the history of England, except perhaps on the single day of Towton in the Wars of the Roses when 33,000 men are said to have been killed.

So I applied for the infantry. Instinct more than thought guided the matter. I was not alone. Others acted in the same way, including Victor Barrington Kent of the Grenadier Guards, Charles Burke of the Royal Irish, and von Pollnitz of the Connaught Rangers; all three were killed, and so were many more.

The first step to joining the infantry was in the pleasant reinforcement camp at Bonaparte's Wimereux, where a dozen of us waited for our orders amid floods of rumours. As a sort of honorary member of our tented Mess we had the very charming society of a young Canadian Army wife, who defied all orders, discipline and regulations to be near her husband, if only in the same country.

The rumours came thicker and indeed more terrible. All was mystery, but some dreadful blow seemed to have struck British, French and Canadian armies alike. The London Division had lost its heavy guns. But the Adjutant General's Office, which was nearby at Boulogne, assured us that all was well, and that no officer reinforcements were presently needed. Naturally I did not believe this, and went to visit the Indian General Hospital near that town. Here I found a ward full of desperately wounded Yusufzais of the 40th Pathans, who had been thrown into a counter-attack. The mystery was solved, and the answer was poison gas.

The enemy had released it secretly from cylinders against the point where the French line met the British near St Jean. The defenceless line broke, but those valiant Canadians stopped the gap, and the 3rd Indian Division were rushed up to counter-attack. Part of this, the entire battalion of the 40th Pathans, was doubling round the ramparts of Ypres city when a storm of heavy shells fell upon them. Eighty of their men fell in a moment, but the rest of the battalion closed its ranks and doubled forward to sustain the attack. The enemy were held, but at very great cost. The half-dozen of us who belonged to this Division refused to listen any longer to the Adjutant General's mandarins, and insisted on railway warrants to take us forward.

A very scratch train carried us in battered carriages nearly to Vlamertinghe, where the civilian driver lost his nerve. He regained it when offered the sharp end of a bayonet. His locomotive suffered from jerks, jibs and refusals, but at last we scrambled off on to the platform which, except for 10 per cent of the booking office, was all that remained of the station. The driver lost not a moment in removing himself and his train to healthier latitudes to the accompaniment of a raucous shout of, 'I will not have my rolling stock destroyed!' from the Rail Transport Officer.

As always when disaster befalls an army, all was confusion. The fog of war was almost worse than the chlorine mists. At last I and Pakenham-Walsh of the Divisional Sappers managed to find an artillery signal party in the cellar of a small café. They contrived a message to our Divisional Headquarters, who sent a car for us. The proprietress of the café was packing up to make a hasty departure, but with the undefeatable spirit of the French managed to give us some coffee, saying, 'No milk, no sugar, only plenty too much scrapnels.' 'Yes,' said the artillery signaller, 'a 5.9 came in just over her bed this morning.'

Soon I found myself in command of a famous regiment of which I had been second junior subaltern only the evening before. Breeks Bainbridge of the 54th Sikhs, handed over to me in a few words: 'We are just going to attack again.' He then broke it to me, not too gently, that only 131 bayonets and one other British officer of the Regiment had survived the division's counter-attack. Six British officers had been killed, including Banks of the Guides.

We marched eastward into the dusk. Behind us came the remains of the Connaught Rangers, the 129th, the Bhopal Infantry and the 4th Londons. We halted and bestowed our weary bones into some wooden huts of indeterminate location; we had no maps. But the efficient and well-ammunitioned German artillery contrived that we should not forget them, putting a steady plastering of 5.9s on to us through the night. In my command, of the sixteen Subadars and Jemadars only three remained, one of them being Mir Dost, an Afridi who received a Victoria Cross for his behaviour on 26 April, and another, Gujar, a Yusufzai of the Guides, who had shown great gallantry.

Then a haggard motor-cyclist brought a message ordering the Regiment once more forward into the attack. The objective was a farm at 16B.5.2, and the 59th Field Battery was to fire in support. It was puzzling because the Brigade and Divisional commanders were well enough aware of what had happened not only to the Battalion but both Brigades as well, which had lost two-thirds of their fighting strength in a couple of hours. It transpired afterwards that Colonel Savy, the gallant commander of the 4th Moroccan Brigade, had informed the Lahore Division that he would assault again at 7 pm on 28 April, and the attack was calculated to fit in.

So the Battalion marched off, with its old-fashioned ammunition carts rumbling behind. As the darkness came down to deepen the murk of shell smoke and mist, we perceived all around us the ghostly glare of Very flames. Strangely enough, no gap could be seen in the ring of rising and falling lights, even towards Vlamertinghe in the narrow gullet of the Salient. No one knew where to find the other brigades, or even the other battalions. After we had spent hours stumbling and slipping on slimy stones on the Flemish road, another messenger overtook us; his despatch countermanded the attack. That was sufficient; all lay down and fell asleep in their tracks. No one thought of food; exhaustion was too great.

In the morning a small lull took place in the roar of the enemy's guns, and the reek cleared away to the north-east. An amazing sight met our eyes. Crowded, axle-arm to axle-arm, on the crest of the Ridge of Grafenstafel there stood, outlined against the sky, a long line of Prussian guns. In the arrogance of overwhelming numbers they scorned the cover of the ridge for the sake of sheer pounding. They might as well have done so; the answering fire of British guns was nil. It was just as well that none of us knew that five days earlier the Germans had broken through the thin

Canadian line on a front of 3,000 yards.

It was a wild scene of desolation and almost of despair. No one knew where the British line held, to keep the enemy from the Channel ports, if indeed it held at all. Shells burst remorselessly everywhere, and the stricken countryside reeked with their smoke and fumes, with which mingled here and there in the hollows, the poison of the mysterious gas, against which there was still no form of defence. All around, dead horses lay, their legs in the air and swollen-bellied. Again orders came for the exhausted band to be thrown into an attack to the north; again this was counter-manded.

We spent the nights of 29 and 30 April in some huts just north of Ypres, and then came orders for the whole of the Brigade to march southwards back into France. Because of enemy air supe-riority this had to be done at night. It was a toilsome march for a number of reasons: the men had not yet recovered from the exhaustion of fighting – many were in some degree still gassed, they were out of training, there having been no practice marches outside the trenches for many months and, an aggravating cir-cumstance, the official rations were inadequate.

At Doulieu came an unexpected but very welcome reinforce-ment of 150 fresh, strong, fit men, who met us at an obscure crossroad. Of these, fifty-three were Punjabis of the Guides, all in new uniforms. Another priceless reinforcement had been the return from hospital of the 57th Wilde's supremely gallant commander, Fred Gray. 'Blast ye' Gray wore that beautiful crimson and yellow medal ribbon gained when our Piffers stormed Peking, and had been severely wounded in the first Battle of Ypres; but that did not abate his lion-like courage or the vigour of his English.

When the Battalion reached its old billets at St Quentin, only a handful of the original men who had landed at Marseilles remained. So great were the losses, especially among British officers that we had to make do with second lieutenants of the Indian Army Reserve of Officers who were not only deficient in military training but completely ignorant of the languages of the fighting regiments of the Punjab. It is incredible but true that the 40th Pathans, having lost every British officer at Ypres, marched south with two second lieutenants who were forced to speak to their men in French.

After an inspection by the corps commander, Lieutenant General Sir James Willcocks, and complimentary messages from Field Marshal Sir Herbert Plumer, no one imagined that the Battalion could be put immediately into another battle, it having come to the limit, so we thought, of human endurance. The High Command had other ideas.

We were to take Aubers Ridge, which on the bloody day of Neuve Chapelle had lain still just beyond our reach. The village of Neuve Chapelle, with its battered brewery, was now firmly in our hold. On a great tossed heap of rubble a huge steel vat lay on its side shot through with hundreds of holes. In the cemetery there had been a tall steel crucifix. Now it was broken, the figure of Christ on the ground but still upright, spattered with bullet splashes.

I was now second-in-command; commander of C Company, of the battalion grenadiers, of its signallers and of its snipers. The company was occupying what we called the Hazara breastwork. It was astonishing to think that this breastwork, which was most beautifully made, was constructed by a company of Afghan subjects, who had come all the way from the centre of that remote country to Flanders to fight for the King of England.

The engagement which has been called the Battle of Aubers Ridge was a tragic bloodbath. When the men of the forward battalions went over they had only eighty yards to go, but in every 100 yards of German front there were many machine guns, in solid concrete emplacements, quite impervious to the poor desultory shrapnel of our artillery, which might as well have stayed at home for all the use they seemed to be. Some Territorial batteries were actually armed with 15-pounders, which the great Lord Haldane did not realize had been out of date at Colenso fifteen years earlier. If their fire gave any results, it certainly escaped our notice.

In a lull during this encounter we fought the small battle of Pope's Nose. Our front line at this point had been an old German support line, from which a Piffer battalion had ejected them in March. Part of this was what we called the Pope's Nose, which had been a communication trench with the remains of a parapet on one side, and shallow shelters on the other. It was within a

60

hand grenade's throw of a bulge in the enemy front line notable for seven fixed periscopes which glared down on anyone crawling about in the mud of this amphitheatre. We had built up the Pope's Nose as best we could to form a listening post, and it was now held by a party of seven Dogras of No.2 Company in front of us, whose task was to maintain our ascendancy in no man's land.

On the second afternoon in this delectable spot the comparative quiet was broken by a heavy bombardment of the Pope's Nose by the enemy's artillery. I hurried up the forward line to meet the commander of the Dogra Company in case the enemy should launch a ground attack. The remains of the picquet were just returning from their sap, and the Havildar was holding a tin periscope with more holes than anyone could count. He told us, maintaining his Rajput aplomb and dignity, that the picquet had been buried, fortunately only lightly, by the first surprise burst and dug out in the nick of time.

The enemy made no move and our casualties were slight, but then Brigade HQ decided to ask us to rebuild our parapet as conspicuously as possible so as to tempt the Westphalians to further effort. He promised us several hundred nice new sandbags for the purpose, and a small party of sappers. In a word, the Pope's Nose was to be converted into a sort of fairground Aunt Sally, and we were to be the pipe in the lady's mouth. Our role was to be shot at. No wonder that when we changed places with the Dogra Company next morning their commander wore a fiendishly pleased expression.

In due course a sapper Havildar and a party of Mahrattas turned up, and the work of rebuilding the parapet proceeded. From late afternoon and through the night the wall of sandbags grew steadily higher. Suddenly a dull report like a cough came from our left front. A few supports seemed to fly straight from the enemy's breastwork; we knew too well what this meant. A few moments later came a thunder-clap, the eye-searing flash, the reek of detonation, and the gasp of the victim. The well-placed mortar bomb was not a thing that one could regard as a trifle, but the stout hearts of the young men brought them back to their toil. We passed the wounded back into the main trench and a second bomb soared towards us. This time the enemy fired a flare from each side of his mortar in order to hide the train of sparks by

61

dazzling our eyes with its glare. This round fell over, but from then on through the night our blood-soaked hole became the very pit of Sheol.

After long endurance in this devil's bowling alley our sandbag task seemed nearly finished. It was nearly dawn and the wall was now high enough to be conspicuous to the enemy, so we crawled back for the morning stand-to. The enemy ignored our obtrusive erection of sandbags until about four in the afternoon, when they blew it to pieces with 5.9s.

But this was not the end of the story. It was up to us to make good the ground and the cluster of craters where our picquet had been. The amphitheatre was wiped out so far as one could see. The vestige of a traverse still remained to mark the junction of the two, and we determined to make this into the best listening post possible.

For shields we had several steel loophole plates of really good quality which we had luckily taken from the enemy a short time before. After dark a small party wormed its way up the trench, scooped out a hollow, and we placed two of the plates on the top of it, covering them with sacking so as not to catch the eye. To protect us were two bombers on duty with a couple of dozen home-made jam tin bombs, which was practically all the Company owned in those penurious days. If the enemy had been worth his salt he should have ventured over, but fortunately he did not.

That afternoon, a load of profanity was seen making its way up what we called 'Hun Street', otherwise our communication trench. This resolved itself into a very young and pink-faced Artillery second lieutenant, brandishing a fine prismatic periscope and accompanied by a sad-eyed bombardier wound round in tangles of telephone wire until he closely resembled a cocoon. When the young officer approached, one of the soldiers began to weep, their experience of artillery support having been somewhat unfortunate in the near past. They even alleged that certain of our batteries were not really on our side at all because at times they seemed to be firing at us – they designated them 'vipers'. The bombardier had difficulty securing telephone communication with anybody who did not curse him violently, but we soothed the youth with some of our rum and communication was effected.

He at last became genial, lost his schoolboy shyness, and we found a suitable spot from which the second lieutenant could observe with his nice new periscope – and then the great idea arrived.

'Tonight we go forth to repair the Pope's Nose,' we told him, as he lapped up the rum. 'We should much like you to fire off a few rounds at the place where the Boche has those two large mortars of his.'

This rather took the bombadier's breath away. The idea of two whole rounds of his precious 18-pounder being thus lightheartedly fired off had staggered him; but the rum did good work. We pointed out that only two rounds were needed; we had located the mortars to an inch, and their emplacement was almost blatantly open.

The shades of night drew on, and more rum came to hand. The Company was once more filling up its sandbags and trickling into the gullet of the sap. Sure enough, there came a lazy whoosh-bang, and two real live percussion shrapnel burst among the enemy's sandbags. The entire German Army seemed to gasp at our impertinence. The Company scurried up the sap, laid its sandbags and was back in the main trench with hardly a shot fired at it. But the sap was only about one-tenth done. We had to give the very young gunner still more rum. This extracted two more rounds.

Visions of what his major would do to him began to swim before his eyes; but the bombardier was bribed with a share of the rum, and again we extracted two more shells. Towards midnight we even procured a couple of high explosives. At dawn the sandbag wall was finished; so was almost six months' allowance of the Battery's ammunition. The listening post was finished, and when our relief came (the 4th Gurkhas) we were able to hand it over to them as good as new.

Soon after this little battle of the Pope's Nose we were relieved and found ourselves at a most pleasant French farm just where the Saint Venant Canal comes out of the Foret de Nieppe.

The Colonel had gone on leave so I was in command, receiving the senior subadars. They told us how considerate they thought the General Sahib was, to give us a few days out of the line just in time for Ramzan. Hardly had they taken their leave when a signal came: we were to go back into the line the next night. Words failed us.

A little later a tall genial figure with red tabs and a gold-rimmed hat stooped through the low doorway.

'Is Blacker in here?'

'Yes, Sir,' said I.

'Well,' he said, 'a cable has just come to Corps Headquarters from the Political Department in India. It says that they want you put under arrest and tried.'

'Oh heavens, Sir; what am I to be tried for?'

'Travelling, my boy,' said he, 'in China without a Chinese passport.'

'Well,' said I, 'in that case I shall not be able to go up to the line tonight', and I offered the GSO a mug of rum.

'But,' he continued, 'the Corps Commander says that no action is to be taken in the matter.'

So that was that, and not many days afterwards one of those highly efficient German gunners decided my future movements.

Chapter 10

THE SYNCHRONIZED GUN

In 1915 the lot of a wounded officer was luxurious to say the least. The wealthiest houses became hospitals, filled with comforts to an almost demoralizing degree. My wounds took about three months to heal, and then a medical board pressed another three months on me, which I hardly deserved. Still, we knew by then that the war was going to last for years, so another three months for physical recuperation was not a matter against which to struggle. The snag came later, when one found that the India Office had been making incomprehensible rules, and, like true bureaucrats, left the victims to find them out for themselves. This particular rule laid down that an officer with more than three months in hospital would not be allowed to go back to his own regiment but would be posted somewhere else.

So I took refuge once more with the Royal Flying Corps, thanks to the good offices of Henry Brooke-Popham. In a flash I found myself called a Staff Captain for Military Aeronautics, with a hutch in 'Zeppelin Terrace', nearest to Heaven in the old War Office, but with *carte blanche* to fly about to the squadrons, even in France. Brooke-Popham's orders were simple and straightforward.

'We must be able to fire our machine guns forward through our propellers. That is your work.'

The great need, in the autumn of 1915, was to find the answer to the Fokker. We needed a 'tractor' aeroplane, with its propeller in front, more efficient and faster; and we needed it armed with Maxim type guns which could fire through its propeller in the best and, to a fighting man, the most instinctive direction, which is straight ahead.

Many were the experiments before we hit on the secret of the 'interrupter' gear. In fact 'interrupter' was a misnomer, as it was intended not to prevent the discharge of a particular bullet which would otherwise hit the propeller (every tenth one in the scheme of the Frenchman, Roland Garros), but to ensure that every bullet went through without hitting it.

Sefton-Brancker's decision to arm pilots with the Vickers gun instead of the Lewis (which was kept for rearward shooting), and the invention of the Scarff-Dibowsky gear for mounting the gun, turned the scale. By December 1915, the Vickers gear had been fitted to our Bristol single-seater fighters with their Gnome Rhône engines in front, and success was not long delayed. Soon our pilots shot down a Fokker, and then some more.

There were other difficulties of course. One was the Government-controlled Royal Aircraft Factory's penchant for putting the observer in front of the pilot, until Pemberton Billing, an active airman, raised Cain in the Commons and forced a Royal Commission under Mr Justice Bailhache which established private enterprise production of aircraft.

Another was the effect of different sizes of engines. The Vickers-Scarff combination worked well with short engines, but large and longer engines took machines to higher and colder latitudes, and the tappet rods which worked the gun gears vibrated, fluttered, shrank and expanded, which caused erratic firing and some propellers to be hit by mistimed bullets. The airman had no parachute in this era, so a split and shivered propeller was a major disaster.

I felt that a hydraulic gear was the remedy and reported thus to Pop Cadell (Brigadier General Walter Cadell, my immediate boss). 'Go ahead and produce one,' he said.

I looked round for a competent designer, and almost at once met one Collie, a major in the new Munitions Inventions Department. He said, 'I want to show you Constantinesco and his trench mortar.'

Georges Constantinesco was a Romanian working with Vickers, and he had invented a gun gear relying partly on hydraulic oil pressure. The mortar itself was not suitable for the army, but the hydraulic system was quite wonderful; not orthodox hydraulic, he insisted, but a wave transmission. This was what the airman needed to transmit the firing impulse from his engine to the lock of his gun without loss on the way, and I jumped at it. Shown the Vickers or Maxim lock, he grasped the problem in a moment, and in nine days his men had constructed the gear, so simple but so completely effective that in the hundreds of thousands that were made no modification was needed, and it continued until the system of mounting eight guns clear of the propeller made it unnecessary.

During all this highly experimental process of finding out how to shoot straight ahead from an aeroplane, I was handed a BE2c to test whether a machine gun could be mounted on the top wing so that it could shoot over the propeller altogether. We installed a Lewis gun there, and I took off at our gunnery school.

No experiment ever fails, as our professor, Bertram Hopkinson, used to say. If it does not show you what you want it to show you, it shows you something else. This was true of this particular experiment, which showed me, when we had dug the nose and engine out of the ground, that the top wing was not the place to put the gun, at any rate not in a low-powered contraption like the BE2c.

When I got out of hospital and RFC convalescent homes my active participation in flying was ended.

Notes:

There is a shot-up propeller belonging to Blacker's aeroplane in Bordon Military Museum, but this was probably not the cause of his crash. More likely it was the reverse rotational force of the machine gun on the top wing of his aircraft, which caused his machine to stall. This problem was not unknown where powerful guns and weak engines were concerned. He crashed into a pond, breaking his neck.

The great value of Constantinesco's invention was that it made the 'interrupter gear' work properly. Mechanical transmission of impulses from engine to firing pin, were not precise enough, at least not in the British version; transmission by hydraulic impulses however, was, and the result was a weapon which worked successfully and reliably throughout the war. Constantinesco received an award of £250,000 for his invention.

Chapter 11

ASSIGNMENT IN ASIA

After a period with balloons, I was passed fit and then posted back to India to command our Training Battalion, where I spent the second half of 1917 despatching drafts of trained and eager recruits to the rebuilt First Battalion in Iraq, who later became part of Allenby's victorious army in Palestine.

I was then summoned to Indian Army headquarters, Delhi. In time, I was ushered into the august but human presence of the Chief of the General Staff, Sir George Kirkpatrick, who told me what was happening in Asia.

Kaiser Wilhelm's ambitions included installing himself as Emperor of India in place of his hated cousin King George V. The Jewish [Russian] Revolution had caused the collapse of the eastern front. The western seas were blockaded, and the Central Powers looked east for supplies of oil, gun-cotton, and men. In the vast territories of Russian Turkestan huge quantities of baled cotton lay waiting in the railway sidings, prevented from going anywhere by the battling of the Red and White Russians. Cotton is an indispensable raw material for the manufacture of smokeless gunpowder and nitro-propellants. We had to stop it being shipped across the Caspian Sea into German hands.

Lenin also had his eyes on India, regarding the British Empire as the chief obstacle to world revolution, and India the source of her power. As soon as it became clear that the workers of Europe were not, as he expected, going to rise against their capitalist oppressors, he turned his face to the East. Moscow's immediate desire was to reinforce the Red Revolution in Tashkent, but their way was barred by a small Cossack army.

Moscow

Orenburg

CASPIAN

SEA

Baku

Enzeli

Krasnovodsk

Bala Ishem

0   300   600 miles

ARAL
SEA

RUSSIAN

TURKESTAN

SEMIRECHENSK

Ashkhabad   Bokhara   Tashkent

KHURASAN

Merv

Andijan

Osh

Shan

CHINESE

TURKESTAN

Irkeshtam

Tien

Meshed

Kashgar   Taklamakan Desert

Yarkand

Pamirs

Herat

Hunza

Gilgit

PERSIA

AFGHANISTAN

Peshawur

Srinagar

TIBET

INDIA

Delhi

Almost limitless manpower was available in Turkestan for any warlord who could provide a soldier with a square meal a day. There had been 180,000 German, Austrian, and Magyar war prisoners there in 1917. During that winter the kindly Soviet, since all were now comrades, released this great mass of trained soldiers, but discontinued their ration supply, so that 90,000 died of typhus and famine. There were fears that the survivors would become a serious menace, which indeed they did, mostly being recruited by the Red Army. Some of them had found their way to Afghanistan, where Osmanli drill-sergeants and Magyar gun-layers lent a new skill to Afghan regiments and batteries. We needed to find out what effect there might be on the Great War from these unchained forces that dreamt of sweeping through the passes of the Hindu Kush to the rich valleys of India.

There was also Enver Pasha to consider. His plan was nothing less than to revive the old Turkish tradition of the White Wolves of Turan and seize all south Asia, not omitting the former Turkish empire of Delhi itself.

So we now faced the prospect of hundreds of thousands hammering at the gates of India whilst Big Bertha was shelling Paris. The Great Game between Britain and Russia had begun again. Our General Staff keenly desired to know what was happening out there, especially to those German prisoners, to all the cotton, to the Red Army, to the Turks, and to the Cossacks.

Three missions were despatched: firstly, a force under Stalky Dunsterville (Dunsterforce) which was already on its way to Baku, but was at the time hotly opposed by Enver Pasha's Turkish army. It took them six months of fighting to reach the Caspian Sea, and so make contact with the second mission. The second mission, under General Malleson, set up headquarters at Meshed in the north of Persia. He had two Punjabi regiments to oppose any forward moves that the newly formed Tashkent Soviet might attempt.

The third, and smallest, was ours to the east in Chinese Turkestan, including Captain P.T. Etherton, Major F.M Bailey, and with Sir George Macartney at its head. We numbered forty shaggy Kirghiz ponies, 160 coolies, and sixteen men of the Guides under Havildar Awal Nur. For reasons best known to themselves the Political Department also sent an expert on Tibet. Perhaps they had not read *The Bad Boys Book of Beasts,* and hence confused the Lama who is Lord of Turkestan with the llama who is a woolly sort of goat 'with a supercilious look and an undulating throat'.

On 20 April 1918 we marched out from Srinagar, with a long train of snow-porters, over the northern passes of Kashmir, still fathoms deep in snow, and after eighteen days arrived in Gilgit. From that hospitable valley the Mission marched up through the remote and rugged valley of Hunza, where it met with a full-blooded hearty welcome in the castle of the Thum. When the time came to leave he provided us with a ceremonial escort.

The Pamirs were reached in about ten days' marching up a narrow valley walled in by stupendous, precipitous mountains. Crossing the Mintaka Pass we met some Kirghiz who had been sent over with yaks to assist our transport to cross the pass. When we halted for breakfast the Hunza men engaged them in conversation. Soon the talk turned to raids, and one of the levies reminded him of the day when Hunza sold six Kirghiz slaves for a single felt carpet. This infuriated the Beg to a frenzy. When he had cooled down a bit, I enquired the cause of his anger.

'The insolence of those Hunza blighters,' he said, 'selling us so cheaply!'

Our escort of Hunza levies passed us on to a scruffy, ungainly guard of Chinese frontier gendarmes, armed with rusty, dirty, single-shot Mauser carbines. They made a sharp contrast with our smartly-dressed, clear-eyed Macedonian offspring, with their dubbined equipment and well-kept, long Lee-Metfords.

Some of our Guides were now mounted on that excellent animal, the western yak. This amiable creature can cover as much ground as a pony, besides being far better on glaciers, moraines and ice-covered rocks, and at very high altitudes. Feroz, my small Punjabi batman, created a world record by making one gallop. This he did with the aid of a sharp HB pencil of mine, to the dismay of the yak's owner.

After Tashkurgan we were greeted with tea and much enthusiasm all along the way. At Yangi Hissar the Chinese militia was turned out with trumpets and banners. The reason for the warmth of the reception was that, although the Bolshevik revolution had been going on for several months, the Cossacks and other Russians posted in this region remained firmly loyal to the Imperial Regime. On 7 June Sir George Macartney rode out from Kashgar with a guard of honour from our new Allies, the Chinese, to conduct us through the streets which were bedecked with flags.

The Mission spent over a month in Kashgar putting itself abreast of the situation. To the east were vast deserts, to the west the political fog of Red Russia. The Iron Curtain had not yet been invented but it was there just the same, and nothing came through it except the odd straggling, struggling, and absurdly optimistic trader. We lingered a while, trusting that some of the fog might blow away; it did not. So we asked Simla for permission to take a small party on to Tashkent and to treat with the Bolshevik government there. In due course the permission arrived.

Etherton stayed in Kashgar to become the new Consul-General, and Macartney stayed with him for the time being. The rest of us rode off through the southern Tien-Shan, a distance of some sixteen marches, to the Russian railhead at Andijan. The intelligence which reached us was of the wildest description. The power of exaggeration amongst the aborigines of those parts is immense. Our little army of sixteen was enlarged by popular report to 60,000. This figure spread over Central Asia and caused some unease to our adversaries.

After Irkeshtam, we rose into higher country in a touch of winter's snow, up to the bone-strewn Terek Pass. At Gulcha we met a solitary Siberian rifleman, who had demobilized himself from his Pamir garrison by the simple process of walking away from it. As most of his comrades and his officers had done the same, one could hardly blame him. A few other Russians were escaping from the Reds into China, including a pretty young school-ma'am, so the night was filled with song and dance.

Two days later we were in Osh, the home of the Emperor Baber, and there we encountered our first Bolshevik commissar. He was the local baker. In spite of his hirsute ferocity and the two pistols in his belt, he did not quite know what to make of us, so contented himself by doing nothing, in typically Russian fashion.

A couple of horse carriages took us from there along the forty miles of fair metalled road into the big electrically lit, cotton-milling town of Andijan, where we met the railway. A few days' stay in an insanitary hotel, staffed by invertebratedly friendly Austrian waiters, brought us into contact with the situation, and incidentally with the Soviet of the town.

Tashkent had been taken almost bloodlessly by the Reds in November 1917. The Cossacks under Dutov, who had taken Orenburg in the same month, took Tashkent back again. But an evil genius prompted them to give the command to a lawyer and they lost their gains within the day. The Cossacks, however, continued to maintain a front across the railway to the north. Fighting with swords and lances, they barred the way to Moscow from Turkestan.

The train to Tashkent was indescribably filthy and crowded. Of course, no Bolshevik would demean himself to clean anything. We found a couple of courteous Chinese merchants and foregathered with them; gentlemanly and well-groomed, they were a contrast to the rest of the human scum that crowded the compartments and corridors. For three days our food was watermelons and the odd tin of sardines.

Our arrival in Tashkent early in the morning of 14 August 1918 was startling both to us and to the Soviet government. To us because, fresh from the Western Front, it gave us a sort of *Alice-through-the-Looking-Glass* feeling to walk in streets full of a jostling crowd, many dressed in the field-grey of the German-Austrian army; to the commissars, because the last thing they expected was a British Mission. Of course, we had to hide the real reasons for our being in their capital, and explain that we were civilian and semi-official to a remarkable degree.

The sensation was intensified in their case when four companies of the Indian Army irrupted into Turkestan in response to an appeal from the Ashkhabad provisional government. The Punjabis, on whom fell the brunt of the hard knocks, as always when Punjabis are in the case, caused us intense joy by tumbling the Red Army into rout. Our joy, however, had to be concealed from the Soviet, who had been receiving wireless messages from Lenin insisting on the early liquidation of all British and French officers. We even had to disown our very good and gallant friends by explaining to the Soviet that they were not His Majesty's troops at all, but pensioners and discharged Afghan subjects who had left the King of England's service, and were fighting purely as

73

mercenaries for the Mensheviks.

The Soviet, by no means a highly educated or enlightened coterie, accepted this explanation, but perhaps this was because they were more afraid of the British government than of fiery demands from the despots of Moscow. Indeed their imagination boggled at the idea of a British Mission coming to an enemy capital in the same week that a British army invaded the country, as well it might.

I remembered 'what a tangled web we weave when first we practise to deceive,' as one of the hospital trains brought back wounded from the Ashkhabad front to Tashkent – amongst others, an Austrian lance corporal. He, with his patrol, had been fallen upon by a patrol of Punjabis and smitten hip and thigh. Though much out of breath, he had managed to escape with a mental picture of the Punjabi soldiers' ragged khaki uniform and accoutrements of the British army. The Red hard core of the Soviet persisted in the notion that a firing squad was the remedy for the problem, and for whatever else was bothering them. My own monocle, to any Marxian mind, was proof that we were emissaries of the capitalist hyenas. One Tobolin, who ran a newspaper called *Sovietski Turkestan*, permitted himself to use some deplorable expressions in our regard. We hoped sometime to meet him alone. The matter became somewhat ticklish, but we managed to make contact with the Austrian lance corporal and sweetened him with some hardly-got beer and palm-oil which caused him to go back on his story; and we breathed again.

The tiny Punjabi force on the Ashkhabad front inflicted defeat after defeat upon the Bolshevik army, and drove them over 200 miles in four months. The Soviet of Turkestan were so perturbed by the reverses suffered by their troops that the mere mention of the word 'Sepoy' made them shudder. In haste they withdrew their crack corps, the 'Zhlobinski Polk', from the Northern front to endeavour to stay the victorious progress of the Punjabis to the south-west.

The Zhlobinskis were mainly composed of ex-convicts, the forgotten exiles of Sakhalin who had been released by the revolutionaries. Even amongst others of the Red Army, who were by no means little Lord Fauntleroys, they were cut-throat swashbuckling ruffians.

74

Their commander, Ginsburg, was one of the very few Hebrews who ever went under fire, and he possessed alone some occult influence over them. He brought them by train into Tashkent. When they arrived they decided to call *en masse* upon the Soviet with a little request for five million roubles – 'None of that Soviet stuff, mind you!'

A prolonged haggle followed seasoned with a few pistollings and at last the Soviet was prized away from the money, with the stipulation that the Zhlobinskis should do as they were told and get off to the Ashkhabad front. They agreed, but two stations south of Tashkent they changed their minds and marched back to the White House for another five million, which they duly trousered.

During the second visit, one of the Zhlobinskis, thinking himself aggrieved in some small matter, decided to call upon the War Minister to obtain satisfaction. He took with him a bellyful of vodka to lend him eloquence, and a stick-grenade to emphasize his arguments. He clambered up the steep stairs of the office, whereupon a chorus of clerks and typists, quite understandably, projected him down again on to the hard, unfeeling pavement. When the broad, cobbled, poplar-lined avenue had ceased revolving, he found the grenade still in his hand and an unoffending local, messing about in the middle of the road in front of him. He decided not to waste the bomb, so withdrew the pin and hurled it at the passer-by. The bomb burst, the stick came back, and with poetic justice killed the thrower. The native remained unscratched.

At last the crack Zhlobinski troops met the Punjabis at the battle of Kaakha, and were cut to pieces. The regiment ceased to exist and their commander died of his wounds. He was brought back to Tashkent for burial, to the genuine regret of the commissars, and a rancour that showed itself in our direction.

Every now and then, when the Soviet decided to remind the citizens who was in charge, an armoured car would hurtle through the streets, its exhaust whistle shrieking, the gunner's thumbs on the buttons of its twin Maxim guns, whilst the cautious got hastily round a corner.

I was more than once roused out of bed at midnight by the fixed bayonets and raucous cry of 'Ruki verkh, tavarish!' – hands up comrade! – from a Red Guard visitation. These episodes seemed like strange dreams.

One night I was pulled up by a heavily armed Red Guard for being out after curfew. He called me 'comrade', and then 'bourgeois,' which annoyed me. I disclaimed the titles, and on his offering me the alternative of dungeon or the bayonet, I told him in my bad Russian that I was a most intimate friend of Sirul, the Commissar of Police, and that if he liked he could come along with me to the police headquarters. He became suddenly quite sober and polite and remarked that it was a fine night for August.

Sirul had a faultless reputation for impressing his wishes on his subordinates, usually with a pistol. He was always very courteous to Sir George and to me, but this cadaverous, pasty-faced, yellow-haired Lett, had a sinister side. One evening, half a dozen commissars of contrary political views were supping in the garden restaurant of our hotel. Without warning, a dozen Red ruffians leapt on them with fixed bayonets, killing a couple on the spot, and dragging the survivors away to the police headquarters, where Sirul had them messily despatched amongst the typewriters and electric fans of his tidy inner office. His explanation to the Soviet, that the deed was done as a kindness in view of the injuries they had received on the way from the restaurant garden, was not very convincing.

We had been six weeks in Tashkent without having been able to get any useful message through to Kashgar, whence it would be sent by runner over the great passes to Gilgit and thence telegraphed to Simla. Some thirty to forty messengers had taken our money and slipped our messages into their great jackboots without tangible results. Doubtless the Reds caught some, and probably courage failed the rest.

One day a pair of our 'White' acquaintances, a man and his wife, offered to take a message for us to Kashgar, which I duly typed. Every few days a train went to the south and east towards the Chinese frontier, and in this they got leave to travel. On the critical evening Sir George and I went to the station to see them off, but were careful not to be conspicuous by going near the carriage. Unfortunately they had been hauled off for searching by a notoriously brutal lackey of the Commissar.

Sir George and I picked our moment and came out of the laurel bushes to lend moral support. I did not know it, but the message was sewn into the servant's long, wadded gown. We were taken to a room to wait among the racks of ancient Vetterli rifles, with mental pictures of firing squads and so forth impressing themselves on our minds. To our relief, Providence guided the police fingers away, and soon we were told to get the hell out of it and not to try any tricks with the Soviet.

However picturesque our adventures might have been had we stayed, it became clear that we could do nothing more in Tashkent towards winning the war. An attempt to install me as one of a Bolshevik Mission to General Malleson failed at the last moment owing to the enemy's suspicions of my bona fides.

Sir George Macartney's announcement to the Soviet of our departure rather upset them. They had an idea of holding us as hostages. The extreme party voted for the dungeon or the firing squad, but the more moderate feared for their own skins if their many enemies should reach Tashkent with British aid. Finally, against their divided counsels, Sir George, by sheer force of his personality, won the day.

I well remember the scene when we discussed the matter with Kolesov, the fanatic Red President of the Tashkent Soviet, in the great rambling White House, whose beautiful teak polished floors ill-matched the frowsy Red Guards who trod them. To the onlooker, it was a wonderful sight to see the mastering, by a superior gentleman, of the unwashed chosen of the proletariat, against their own desires. So complete was the victory of the higher mind, that the Soviet even gave us a special train.

But we had not yet finished with the conspiratorial complex of the Reds. In Tashkent itself the Soviet's nerves had failed in the matter of arresting us. But when we arrived at Andijan, early in the morning when nobody was about, we were pounced upon by a rough, shaggy-looking patrol of military police, commanded by a Galician. The truculent tone and manner of this wretch made it clear to us that he had telegraphic instructions from the Tashkent Soviet to double-cross us.

These official ruffians were not very clear about their own instructions, or what their superiors intended them to do; but they took every opportunity to flourish the points of their bayonets just short of our abdomens.

Once more we renewed our acquaintance with the business end of the slim, quadrangular Russian bayonet, 1906 pattern. It differs from other bayonets in the world. It has four even faces and a square-sectioned point, so that it may serve also as a screwdriver, not that the recipient is likely to feel it more comfortable on entry. It has no scabbard and is always kept fixed, maintaining the ancient Suvorov tradition.

These official thugs became much flummoxed by the amount of rubber-stamped paper which we showed them. Then we pulled the 'extra-territoriality' card. This seemed to be a word which was too long for them. Their chief stammered that they must show this to the Soviet. This passing of the buck seemed very welcome to them, and, as they hurried off into the town, I jumped out, secured a droshky, and in a very few minutes we were galloping off to the Chinese frontier.

Chapter 12

A DASH THROUGH THE
MUZTAGH

In about twenty marches, moving by little-known short cuts, we had got back to the Chinese Pamirs, where most of my soldiers, after some adventures of their own, had managed to concentrate. This was the end of September 1918, and news of an impending German break-up in the West had filtered through to Central Asia, and German agents in North Afghanistan were on the move.

We got news at Tashkurghan that an armed party of some 200, comprising Germans, Turks, and Afghans, had moved across from the Russian Pamirs down the wild, menacing gorge towards Yarkand. I gave chase with eight of my own men and seven of the Orenburg Cossacks, and after three days and three nights of scrambling over cliff faces and marching in almost untrodden valleys, found that we were on the wrong trail. Meanwhile, Sir George had pushed on towards India to put the results of the Mission's work into the hands of the Foreign Office as quickly as possible. My little force overtook him a couple of marches farther on, at a place called Dafdar, where we struck a fresh trail. I received orders to follow this trail leading up into the desolate, uninhabited valley of the Oprang, which abuts on to the greatest mountain barrier in the world. If I came on any definite signs, I was to follow the trail and capture the party that made it, since it was quite clear that no one but enemy agents would use such a route. Sir George continued towards India, and I exchanged the Cossacks for half a dozen deep-chested, iron-limbed men of the

Hunza Scouts. We pushed on and up into the snow, a long march, to a couple of tiny tents, where the wife and sister of a wandering shepherd awaited the gathering of their flock to proceed to more genial climes at lower levels. That night the two girls confirmed the midnight passage, seven or eight days before, of fifteen mounted armed men. We followed them over the very difficult Ilisu Pass in snowstorms, crossing ice-bound rock faces and snow-fields, upon which their tracks unmistakably showed; then two days down the long valley to the great Yarkand River. We just managed to ford the swollen river without loss, and then began a series of mighty passes. We crossed six of these in four days, only one of them under 16,000 feet, whilst one or two had snow cornices on their summits and sheet ice on their slopes which killed several of our wretched ponies. We had no kit beyond the clothes the men stood up in, their sheep-skin cloaks and saddle blankets, plus a small bag of flour and tea in their wallets. Some of our bivouacs were waterless, fuel-less, and devoid of grazing, in holes scraped in the snow, in open valleys at 14,000 feet. At last, having seen no living thing for several days, we dropped down from the great height into the brushwood-filled valley known as Kulan Aghil, where we found human beings and secured a bag of flour and a sheep just in time to stave off star-vation. Better than this, even, we had caught up four days on the enemy, who, strangely enough, instead of marching straight into Yarkand over a single pass, turned sharply to the eastward into the great unknown, unmapped valley of Chup. We followed them, exchanging our worn-out ponies for some fresh animals belonging to a few Kirghiz whom we met. We had long been down to one meal a day, cooked on flat stones, at the short midday halt, since we had neither time nor food for more. From Chup we climbed over a great weird pass into the equally unknown valley of Bulun, where in a hamlet we learnt that we were now only forty-eight hours behind the pursued. Unfortunately here we lost the track and had to make a nightmare march through four great unmapped passes, of which I never even found the names, since we met no human being to tell us, in all those great valleys and deep, cliff-walled canyons. On that one day, I estimate that we climbed up and down 30,000 feet.

At a little clump of deserted huts in a waterless valley named

Yarkand

Khan Langar

Muztagh Ata
24,388

Tashkurgan
10,280

16,000

Yarkand River

Tiznaf River

Tashkurgan River

Dafdar

to India

Kulan Aghil

Chup

Bulun

Ak Masjid

Ilisu

Oprang

17,000

16,000

15,600

17,000

17,100

14,500

16,000

M U Z T A G H

R A N G E

0   10   20   30   40 miles

= route

after the Archangel Gabriel, we were still off the trail. Our first drink for forty-eight hours was given to us by a woman at Ak-Masjid; it was one of those drinks one never forgets. A very few hours' sleep and then a night march by compass over a sandy range into the next valley of Tiznaf; then a long nightmare march through the whole of the day and the whole of the night took us to Khan Langar, where we again met the mighty Yarkand River where it debouches into the plain.

Now at last we came out of the immense, heaven-reaching mountains and across the desert to the great ancient city in its high-towered walls, Yarkand, where I had been before in 1914.

Before the sleepy inhabitants of the narrow alleys of the city knew what was happening, we had cantered inside the walls and thrown open the great iron-studded gates of the Badakshi Sarai.

1. Flying licence No.121.

2. Stewart Blacker getting out of a Be2a.

EAST OF NEUVE CHAPELLE

3. Aerial photograph east of Neuve Chapelle 1915.

4. Testing the synchronized gun.
(*IWM Q66258*)

5. NCOs of Blacker's detachment Turkestan 1918. *From left:* Baz Mohammed, Kalbi, Feroz, Ahmad Shah, Awal Nur, Abdullah Shah.

6. Summit of Mintaka Pass May 1918, Rashid Beg and Blacker centre, Hunza scouts on right.

7. A Patrol of guides mounted on yaks.

8. Punjabi machine-gunners.

rters crossing the Tragbal in March
18 on the way from Gilgit to Kashmir.

10. Victim of the Persian police at Meshed.

Tekke Turkoman and his wife.

12. Kalbi and Awal Nur dressed in Bokharan robes, with Bailey.

13. Armoured train on the Annenkoff front, Russian field gun visible.

4. Captain Blacker on Marushka 1919. *From left:* Old Ashraf, Baz Mohamed, Ahmad Shah, Blacker, Jahan Dad, Feroz, Nazar, Amal Baz, Awal Nur, Aslam, Ivan Valkovitch.

5. In Bajgiran. *From left:* Blacker, Kutumbiah, Miss Houston, Duffy, Captain Duncan. Miss Houston had just made a dramatic escape from Tashkent.

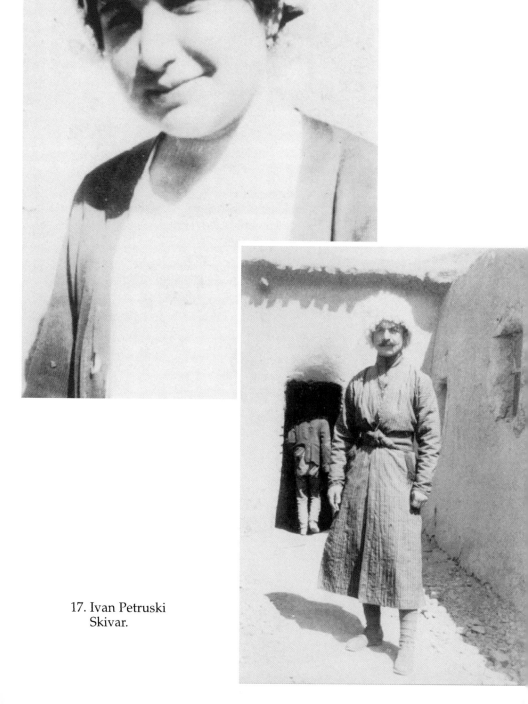

16. A Bolshevik spy.

17. Ivan Petruski
Skivar.

8. A Hazara and three Persian levies.

19. Crossing the
Batura Glacier.

20. Insignia of major general in the Red Army offered to Stewart Blacker after the siege of Jiristan.

21. Unloading a Westland at Karachi.

2. Aeroplane with elephants.

3. Mount Everest through the stays from 2½ minutes distance.

24. The summit of Everest.

25. Dame Fanny
Houston.

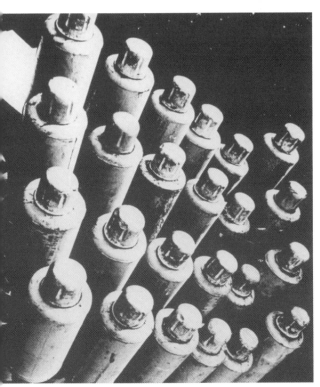

26. The Hedgehog.

27. Blacker Bombard.
(*IWM H12300*)

28. Tank armed with
    Petard projector.
    (*IWM H38003*)

29. Petard bombs.
    (*IWM H36609*)

and 31. The PIAT.

32. View from
    behind a 2″
    thick steel plate
    showing the
    effect of five
    shots from PIAT
    shells fired at
    an angle of 45°.

33. The effect of
    blast and
    splinters on ¹/₁₆
    inch steel plate
    placed 1ft
    behind the 2″
    plate.

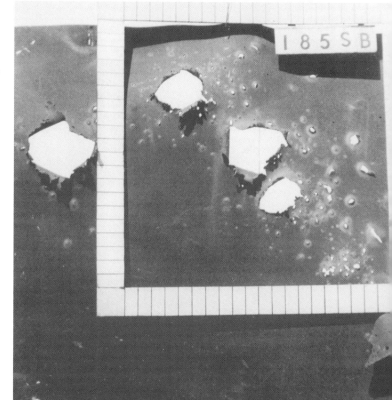

Chapter 13

YARKAND TO MERV

At last, after all our desperate toils, our quarry was in our grasp. The Afghans were struck so dumb with amazement by this bolt from the blue that foiled all their plans and hopes, that no hand was raised to strike a blow against us. One great deep-chested, black-bearded Bajaouri, in the rich gold-laced velvet coat that marked him as a leader, sank down with his head on his knees, burying his face in his hands. So plain was his misery that the soldier standing over him, touched by it, withheld the bayonet prod that he had earned to make him keep his hands above his head.

To our great disappointment there was no German in the party – a cruel stroke of luck after what we had been through. The whole wild adventure seemed like a nightmare, and I am convinced that we could never have carried it through except for a sort of moral exaltation that lifted our minds away from bitter cold, hunger, and the extremes of bodily exhaustion.

However, we were comforted by knowing that we had obeyed our orders and carried out our task: we felt that no one could have done more. I was grateful to Providence that, close though things had been, all the men had been brought through alive: a mistake in direction, or even a piece of bad luck, would almost certainly have cost the lives of the whole party. Had I not learnt it already in the hard schools of Neuve Chapelle, of Ypres, and before the Aubers Ridge, I would now have realized a little of the gallantry and unswerving devotion of the Punjabis and Pathans with whom it was my privilege to serve.

It took us some hours to put each of the principal men separately through his interrogation and to ransack their effects. Their arms, Austrian rifles and bayonets, and the markings on them, showing the Royal and Imperial Regiments they had come from, were of the most interest. Meanwhile a great crowd of the goitrous offscourings of mid-Asia collected in the alleys outside, and were kept from the gates by the ready rifle-butts of a couple of my men.

In the middle of it all trumpets sounded in the streets, and a richly-dressed man rode up with a dozen cavaliers, asking what it was all about. He was brusquely admitted and explained that he was the Bong-Bong, the diplomatic secretary to the Amban of Yarkand. He displayed some excitement about what was going on.

However, remembering that in case of trouble my sixteen bayonets were more than a match for the whole Chinese army in that region, and not forgetting the advice of the dear old Thum of Hunza, always to ride the high horse with the Chinese, I told him icily that *inter arma silent leges* [he who has the weapons makes the laws] though this took a good deal of translating into Jagatai Turkish. I added that when I had quite finished, I would let the Amban know the upshot of the matter. This made the Bong-Bong pause to cogitate, whereupon young Kalbi, with the ready resource that is a tradition of his Corps, told him that I was the commander of 2,000 soldiers back in Mardan, and addicted to shooting first and arguing afterwards.

Then Kalbi remembered that I would need some Chinese visiting cards. He pressed a few coins into the gorgeous Bumble's hand, and commanded him to hurry off and get some printed in the city. The town clerk reeled away, very flustered, with the bewildered expression that one might expect to see on the face of the Lord Mayor of London's assistant if a savage-looking Mongol soldier were suddenly to thrust some coppers and an errand upon him.

The visiting cards materialized in due course, bearing the name 'Ber-Lak-Erh'. It was essential for one's name to take up three syllables, persons of two syllables being of no consequence.

The prisoners were soon well and truly chained up. We marched out with them between armed men and the gaping faces of the teeming, astonished crowd, to our billet. In this, a strongly shuttered room, was their abode, with a Hunza sentry over the doorway.

The Amban sent his cards over with an invitation to lunch on the morrow. The next morning we spent several frantic hours sprucing ourselves up, collecting an ancient cobbler from out of the city to cobble some more clouts of yak hide to our gaping boots.

I left a guard over the prisoners and took the rest of the men, with buttons and bayonets well polished, and clothes and boots mended as best possible, to the first of the sevenfold heavily carved portals of the Yamen. They made a brave show, and as they were all well-grown lads, quite overshadowed the somewhat scraggy Chinese guard of honour that presented arms with a roll of drums.

The ceremonial opening of the gates took place to the noise of loud salutes fired from squat 'Coehorn' mortars. These the Amban's guards discharged by the simple process of placing hot embers within and throwing powder bags on the top of them from a not-too-safe distance. Anyhow the bangs were very satisfying, and before long we were sitting down to enjoy the most courteous hospitality of the old Chinese Mandarins, which is not to be excelled anywhere at all, and supported by a delicate and cultured cuisine. The detachment had a hearty spread next door, along with the officers of the Chinese garrison. In the Yamen there were several criminals serving their sentences, some in cages, and one with a log of wood chained to his neck and ankle.

Out host was enthralled by stories of the War in the West, especially when I told him of my experiences in the Flying Corps. He remarked that he thought that I ought to have been in the Submarine Service. The joke took a little understanding until I remembered that in Turkish *balik* means fish, and that my Chinese card, lying by his plate, read 'Ber-Lak-Erh'. This pleased him a good deal, so we all laughed immoderately. Lunch ran to over thirty courses.

The wine circulated, and at last the business of the prisoners, casually mentioned as an afterthought, became easy. In fact our host became most cordial, and even went so far as to lend me four mounted gendarmes to save my tired men some of the fatigue of escorting the prisoners to Kashgar.

We marched out next day with our prisoners, under the great ramparts of the city, accompanied for a few miles by a couple of score of the British subjects doing business in Yarkand, who, being up against the hard facts of the world, realized a little of what they owed to the soldier.

Our next move was clearly to get back to India as soon as we could in order to rejoin our battalions. The men, who had had a few good square meals of fresh mutton, ample fruit, and the round half-leavened buns of the Yarkand bakers, looked far fitter. I knew the road well, having marched along it in 1914. But the days were short, and our horses were still tucked up, so we had to march till the early hours of the morning.

Etherton and the Russians were a little surprised to see us when we suddenly appeared in Kashgar, booted and spurred, after two and a half days' marching from Yarkand. The business before the house was firstly, of course, the disposal of the prisoners. This meant a State visit to the Do-Tai's yamen, and a lunch with the hilarious old man, who rather, to my mind, resembled a Deal boatman. When it came to the crux of handing over the fettered Afghans to the Chinese, I felt a little twinge of remorse: there was something unnatural in giving Aryans, ruffians and enemies though they were, into the hands of an alien race. The old Do-Tai was genuinely appreciative of the labours of the detachment, so next day he turned up with an immense bag of silver, so heavy that one man could scarcely lift it, and he proposed to distribute this to the men. It took a good deal of tactful explanation to make him understand that our men were above receiving tips for doing their duty, but he took it in good part, and carted the bag back to his yamen.

A dozen fresh horses raised, we were just heading off on our long march towards India when a runner came in from Gilgit with news from the Western Front. It was not very up to date, but gave us an idea that the end of the Germans' resistance was not far off. We all felt disappointed that we were going to be 'out of it' again. I little dreamt there were several more wars ahead of us.

We returned to the Pamirs by the Gez route: though it is the shortest, it is a vilely rough track. After a long and weary march we reached the little fort of Langg-Tai on the Chinese frontier. We were now in the sphere of the Pu-Li Amban who had behaved discourteously to Sir George in October on his way from Kashgar to India, and had caused us trouble in the past.

The Langg-Tai post has a garrison of one decrepit Kirghiz, and would be untenable against a barrage of well-aimed brickbats. It has, however, more than once loomed large in *Welt Politik*. The Quai d'Orsay, Downing Street, and the Nevski Prospekt, used to contemplating Gibraltar, Ehrenbreitstein, or Kronstadt, could not visualize an Imperial Chinese Fortress, 'where three empires meet', as being an edifice unsafe to lean up against.

Riding up to the fort, in a gentle drizzle of wet snow, I asked the Kirghiz sentry where the Da-Ring was. He replied, rather shamefacedly, that the latter was sick, and inside the fort. Suspecting nothing, I gave him my card and a message to the Da-Ring, telling him not to trouble himself to come out to receive me, if he was unwell. The sentry, in a rather off-handed way, pointed to some tents for us. I tied up my horse to the lee of one, and going inside found a young Kirghiz damsel within. We smiled sweetly at each other across the brushwood fire in the middle of the tent.

Meanwhile the men had settled themselves down, so I went to enquire about the matter of firewood, and a sheep, and some barley for the horses. I met the sentry again who had since been to the Da-Ring, and he answered curtly that there was nothing for us here, and that we should go up a side-valley, several miles off our route where the Beg of the tribe there would give us supplies. This surprised me, for the Kirghiz make an almost religious duty of hospitality, and offer any traveller everything he wants as a matter of course. I concluded that I had misunderstood him, so I went back into the tent to find Feroz and the Kirghiz girl billing and cooing together, and making tea.

Suddenly into the gloom of the tent there lurched a villainous, squat Mongol figure with great ridged eyebrows like Attila: an animal face distorted with rage. A sheepskin cap was over his eyes, he was muffled in a long, greasy sheepskin robe, and he trampled over my blankets in his great jackboots to launch a torrent of gibberish at Feroz, whilst the girl shrank terrified into a corner. Feroz, though half his size, eyed him with contempt and returned few quietly incisive remarks in Punjabi. These did not wither the Mongol, as well they might not, since he did not understand them. Instead he grappled with young Feroz, who, nothing loath, landed him a shrewd dunt on the chin, followed by a cross-hook to the jaw and a straight left to the mark. Thus overwhelmed, the burly Mongol collapsed on to his hands and knees. Feroz followed up his success with the violent impact of a well-nailed ammunition boot to the hinder end of the intruder, who was soon bleeding profusely in the cold snow outside.

In a twinkle the fair Kirghiz was suffused in smiles as she turned her admiring face towards the bashful Feroz. Within moments another Kirghiz hurried in with a great bundle of firewood, then another followed with a huge bowl of milk, and then bags of barley began to appear as if from nowhere. Next, the sentry led up a fat sheep, with a very different expression on his face from that which had adorned it ten minutes before (the sentry's face, not the sheep's, who no doubt anticipated becoming mutton very soon). All this seemed somehow connected with the chastisement of the ugly one, so I enquired from the lovely Kirghiz who he might be. In a hushed tone she said: 'He is the Loya.'

A Loya, apparently, was a Chinese military dignitary, and by no means an unimportant one. Here was another bush of thorns. I foresaw myself butchered to make an ambassadorial holiday, in an international incident. The Chinese are very touchy about having their soldiers knocked about, probably because they so often need it.

As I drank the tea I cogitated, and the worthy Thum's advice came into my head again: I decided to take the initiative, and to ride the high horse. I sent the sentry to tell the Da-Ring that I wanted to see him at once. The sentry came back repeating that the Da-Ring was sick and could not come. So I sent the invaluable Kalbi, who had a way of achieving results, to bring the Da-Ring to me and to brook no refusal. In a few minutes he came, in his best uniform, wearing his sword, closely followed by Kalbi, who looked as if butter would not melt in his mouth. We politely told him to sit down by the fire and to take a cigarette. He did so, and rather heatedly began to declaim about the manhandling the ugly Loya had received.

Coldly I remarked that this was not why I had sent for him, but to demand an apology in the matter of the Loya having laid his hands on Feroz. He stuttered that the Loya was senior to Feroz in rank, with a detachment of sixteen soldiers under him, so he could not make him apologize. I replied that Feroz was also the commander of sixteen. At this Feroz stifled a guffaw. He knew as well as I did that twelve of those sixteen were mules, since he was a transport driver. I added that if I did not get the apology at once, I would put the Loya under close arrest and take him myself under escort to the Pu-Li Amban. The Da-Ring began to have visions of his head falling into the sawdust, and Kalbi improved the occasion by recounting an imaginary experience of his, wherein a Chinese mandarin was decapitated for churlishness to a 'foreign devil'. At last the Da-Ring decided he himself would apologize, as the Loya was too sick to do so. I retorted that I would not take an apology from him, with whom I had no quarrel, but insisted on a personal meeting with the Loya. Eventually he told me that the Loya would apologize in the morning. This was good enough, so we gave the Da-Ring some tea and cigarettes, and parted friends.

Early next morning I went into the fort with Kalbi, to meet the now sycophantic Kirghiz sentry. The sentry explained that the Loya was still asleep in a little room under the fort wall. We went there, to find a stove nearly red-hot and an immense pile of sheepskins on a platform by the wall; from under this came snores. The air was nearly solid, so we kept the door open, and gusts of snow-laden air came swirling in. Prodding the heap produced no result, so the sentry was made to haul the sheepskins off. The biting blast produced a sort of consciousness in the brute-like figure that now groaned. It was in a thin cotton shirt, so the fresh air had the maximum effect. A few brief words explained the object of our visit, which only produced more groans, so the sentry was made to prop up the battered hulk and to prize open the contused eyes with his fingers. He seemed to like causing pain to his superior officer.

When the Loya saw the fixed bayonet of Kalbi and his uncompromising face, he began to realize that things were serious, and he stammered out an apology in Chinese. The sentry was made to nudge him again, and at last his bruised lips framed an apology in Turkish. We slammed the door and left him to his frowst, happy in the thought that in the event of a diplomatic incident, he had acknowledged himself, before witnesses, to be in the wrong.

That was a load off my mind, but the next trouble was the bitter Arctic climate, and the fact that the hospitable Kirghiz had moved away into warmer valleys, and we could no longer stay with them in their tents.

After a long march we were lucky enough to find a couple of Kirghiz tents under the lee of some rocks, and we were glad enough to get out of the blizzard. Next day we reached Tashkurghan, for the fourth time that year, and somehow avoided having an open row with the Pu-Li-Amban.

After Tashkurghan the weather became even worse, and to add to our troubles influenza appeared. We had picked up a few men of the Hunza Company of Scouts at Tashkurghan, who had been living in houses for some time, and no doubt they collected the germ for distribution to my own men.

Every man of the detachment except myself and my orderly were attacked by it, but with the very great fortitude that I had come to expect from them as a matter of course, they all continued to ride their horses through the very long marches we were compelled to make. Imagine yourself, dear reader, who scurry to a warm bed, with an eiderdown over you, a blazing fire, and a jorum of toddy, when you feel a bit queasy, compelled to force nerve and sinew to sit on a rough Kirghiz pony for twelve or fourteen hours a day, over a stark, frozen plain, with the thermometer way down below zero, in a howling, biting wind, and with a single torn blanket to wrap yourself in when you reached the shelter of a ragged cave under a rock.

This was part of the calamitous influenza epidemic which killed more people than the Great War itself. Many of the Sarikolis lay dead in their homes, and I believe that it was only the Spartan conduct of my men that saved more than one death in the detachment. Had we halted to nurse a case, the germ, which seemed to flourish under the shelter of a roof, would only have had fuller scope to do its deadly work.

At last we came to Payik, where the broad, swift river was frozen over with nearly three feet thick ice, and the leg of a sheep that Feroz carried slung on his saddle for the evening meal froze solid at midday. The altitude here is about 14,000 feet, and the cold blast blows straight from between the worlds. At night the planets and stars, no longer walled off from man's sight by the turgid layer of the lower atmosphere that oppresses plains-living mortals, blazed like young suns from a jet-black vault over the universal mantle of snow and ice, pierced here and there by cliffs and pinnacles of iron rock.

The crossing of the Mintaka was abominably cold. When we got down to lower levels, a night in a half-roofed sheep-pen between the great cliffs of Murkushi seemed almost stuffy in comparison, even at 12,000 feet.

After crossing the primeval green ice-cliffs and hummocks of the great Batura glacier, nearly a mile wide, our next halting-place was at Gircha, where at last, after many weeks, we slept on beds, with a complete roof over our heads. This was in the house of a hospitable old uncle of the Thum's, who had, for some misdemeanour, been banished to this out-of-the-way village.

Next day we met the Thum, who received us like old friends. I got on to his telephone to the Political Agent at Gilgit. The great news came down the wire, 'The Germans have signed an armistice'.

The War had been over a good many days, and we were already starting to lose the peace. I thought of the day way back in 1914, when I was also in remote Turkestan, on which I heard of the outbreak of the War. We did not know whether to be pleased or not, for to tell the truth every one of the Regulars wanted to be back with the regiment, hammering the Turk, and giving back a few of the hard knocks that we had received in the bloody days of 1915 and 1916.

To cheer us up we spent all day playing polo, galloping, as the Hunza men do, the steel-wire Badakshi ponies on the rock ground.

Two days more saw us back in Gilgit and complete civilization. We got some money here, and some socks and boots, and were soon on our way back over the Burzil and the Tragbal into Kashmir. We had more trouble with the influenza at Astor, since we needed snow-porters, and the epidemic had laid them all out. At last we got enough to go on with; but soon they gave us trouble, sinking down in the snow and refusing to go on. When one or two weak ones were left behind some miles out in the snow, the more robust objected strongly to go back to help them in. Their objections were overruled.

91

From Rawalpindi the men went off on leave. I went on to Delhi to hand in my reports, and to draw maps of the unexplored country we had traversed.

Meanwhile events had been moving in Turkestan: Merv had been taken by our troops after bloody fighting, and we hoped soon to advance to the Oxus, and on to free Tashkent and the whole of Turkestan from the Red yoke.

I had not been more than a few days in Delhi before I received an invitation to betake myself to the Merv front. Of course, I jumped at it, as my battalion was now doing peace-time duties at Baalbek.

I decided to take my old and trusty band with me, and we all met again, girded for war, on the platform of the loopholed station at Lahore. Christmas Day of 1918 was spent in the train travelling through the desert to Quetta.

Before leaving I had had difficulty in getting fresh clothing for my men, especially greatcoats. However, men on leave and the sick from British units had been coming back in large numbers to India, from Mesopotamia, where they had received excellent clothes with brass buttons. Many of these they sold to obtain money for beer. So, driving back one day from the clothing depot after an unsuccessful quest, Awal Nur and I came upon a party of Brahui labourers, nearly all wearing excellent greatcoats, with beautiful brass buttons. We both had the same idea at once. Pulling up, I asked the leading labourer whether he knew that it was a criminal offence to be in possession of Government clothing. His jaw dropped and he goggled blankly. I invited them all to accompany me to the court of the civil authority, who would be glad to send them to jail for a period of years. Awal Nur added a few artistic and convincing details. The Brahuis were aghast: escape was impossible, so they threw themselves on my mercy. My hard heart was at last melted by their prayers, and I consented to take over the greatcoats, and say no more about the matter. Awal Nur made himself very nearly ill with laughing when he told the rest of the men how we had got greatcoats for them.

It took us two more days and nights to get to the end of the railway, which broke off abruptly in the desert, by a clump of tents. We were left with a 700-mile march.

The first half was hot and arid. At Birjand we exchanged our camels for a wagon, and got rid of a mass of coolies. By the time we got to Meshed it was cold and drizzly. We spent a few days there, and marched off again to the front at Merv: the fourth time that I had entered Turkestan from other countries, though never without a thrill of what the future would hold.

We took a little-used mountain track that crossed the Kara Dagh and led us, in four marches, to the railway. As we came down the valley of the Garm Ab which rises in a hot spring, the snow and mist cleared away and a wonderful sight confronted us. This was the rock wall formed by the inner scarp of the range that, running in a dead straight line, divides Persia from Turkestan. About 500 feet of sheer cliff springs up from the undulating downs pierced only by a few narrow gorges where streams have forced their way through. It has for centuries kept warlike Mongol, Turkoman and Uzbek, not to say Russian, from getting at the convivial and engaging Persian as forcibly as they would like. As we marched into Qaratigan, there towered the miracle of Khorasan, the stupendous rock fortress Kelat-i-Nadiri.

Next day we came over a few hills to the gorge of Haji Bulan. Here was a customs house, and the polite Persian customs man invited us to an excellent meal of *oeufs à la coque* and entertained us with stories of life in Tehran – the city he longed to go back to. Just as we were going to bid him goodbye, he broached the subject of paying customs dues on our kit that was coming along on mules. The idea of an armed party, on its way to join a force fighting in the neighbourhood, having to pay customs to leave a country that it did not want to stay in, seemed rather laughable. However, we could not very well shoot the lad, as we had been his guests – in any case, it would have been rather Prussian; so we parleyed. At length, like a true bureaucrat, he consented to waive the matter as long as we would give him a 'writing'. So that was that: His Majesty was let in for half a crown on a paper IOU, and marched off through the gorge, accompanied by the polite customs man on a squealing stallion and a few of his Turkish preventive men.

Outside the frowning scarp that walls in Khorasan, smiling downs, green with the first promise of spring, rolled down to the immense plain, and we cantered easily along the grassy cart-track. It was still daylight when we trotted over the rank grass of the battlefield of Dushak, where in September the Reds had been badly cut up by our troops. Skeletons littered the ground, mixed with empty cartridge cases, that showed us where a squadron of the 28th Light Cavalry, taking advantage of such an opening as every cavalryman prays for, had speared a thousand Bolsheviks.

A couple of miles on lay Dushak village, its white-washed cottages still splashed with shrapnel ball and nickel-jacketed bullet, and as dusk fell we rode to the station. A train came in after dark and we clambered on board. Our horses went into a couple of trucks, and we all scrambled into a fourth-class wagon such as is used to take emigrants to Siberia. Waking up in the morning, we found four British soldiers of the 9th Warwicks had been in already. They had already established an *entente* with Abdullah Shah and Aslam, and were making tea in a great tin for the public benefit. All through the War I have noticed how British soldiers, when they are real fighting infantry or gunners, are always ready to make friends with Pathan, or Punjabi soldiers in particular.

Chapter 14

RAILWAY WARFARE ON THE MERV FRONT

Before long we got to Merv, and at Bairam Ali, a dozen miles east, we found Brigade Headquarters installed in the palace of the Emperor, a summer residence in the midst of his estate. Kipling's allusion to the dream of every British soldier of the eighties – 'cooking their camp-kettles in the palace of the Tsar' – was now fulfilled. It was to my platoon of the Corps of Guides, now attached to the force, that the honour fell.

The Bolsheviks on this front had been severely damaged whilst we were in Tashkent parleying with their Soviet. But so had the Punjabis: at Dushak the whole brunt fell on the 19th who lost 50 per cent of the effectives and all their British officers, and on the 28th who had charged the Bolshevik Magyar infantry over the grassy downs.

The victory of Dushak reflects no little credit on the troops engaged: separated by 800 miles from their railhead, enduring the bitter cold of the 'drear Chorasmian wastes' in khaki cotton drill, rationed on what they could pick up in the barren country, deficient of Lewis guns, grenades, and everything that one is accustomed to associate with modern war – they attacked and routed ten times their number of trained, well-found European troops, lavishly armed with abundant quick-firing artillery and dozens of machine guns. Almost without a pause they drove them back 200 miles to Merv – a great achievement, the fame of which resounded all over Central Asia.

During the intervals between these fights the little force had developed from the band of insurgents out of which it had grown. The real fighters were the 19th and 28th, backed by some Russian guns, mounted on armoured trains. There were a couple of regiments of Turkoman horse and a battalion of foot, more apt for looting than fighting. Afterwards a squadron was formed of loyalist Russians, trained or armed by us. Finally a section of 18-pounders of 44 Battery RFA reached us, whilst a British company did duty on the lines of communication in Ashkhabad.

The armoured trains had been a prominent feature of operations from the beginning. Our artillery was mounted on railway trucks, and protected either by steel plates or by bales of cotton compressed for shipment. The gun crews lived on other coaches on the train which usually mounted a machine gun or two on the roof, while the infantry and cavalry were lodged in separate unarmoured trains.

The Bolsheviks had a similar arrangement, except that the moral atmosphere of their trains left a good deal to be desired. In fact, to say that the males and females therein lived like beasts would be an affront to beasts.

The single line ran for hundreds of miles of the Kara Kum Desert, amongst sand dunes some twenty to forty feet high. It soon became clear that it was necessary to have a bend in the line in order to fight a battle or to make a stand. When one side attacked, it was usual for them to open the action by steaming round the bend out from the cover of the sand hills, all guns blazing. The infantry would attack over the desert, whilst the cavalry operated thirstily on the flanks.

If the Bolsheviks were defeated and had to flee down a straight stretch of railway, they could not make a stand until the line formed a bend again, which would give cover for their armoured train.

To the civilized Westerner, accustomed to regard a railway as a sort of unerring mechanical brand of Providence, it was a strange sensation to have a complete broad-gauge modern railway at one's beck and call, with whole trains and locomotives to play about with and to blow up.

A favourite way to irritate the Russians in these operations was the time-honoured jest of blowing up the line in rear of their trains. To do this a half-squadron of our non-regulars would

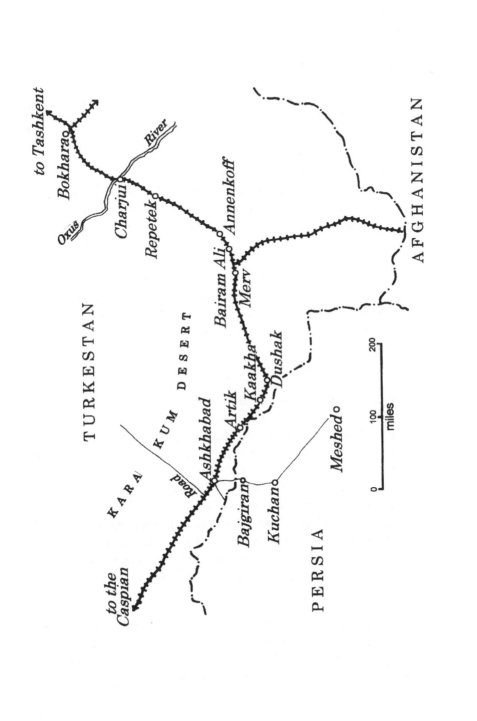

provide itself with some gun-cotton, and proceed on a long, weary, and very thirsty detour across the dunes of the desert for many miles until they reached the line behind the enemy. The rest was easy, except that the return journey was usually even thirstier than the outward.

Before long a bright brain realized that a contact mine left under a rail offered a far better result for the trouble expended, in that one could hope thus to bag a gun-truck. The counter to this was the placing of an empty truck or two in front of the leading gun-truck to take the force of the explosion.

The attackers were again driven to put on their thinking-caps and devised a mine that only responded to the tender caress of something weighing several tons, such as a gun or a locomotive. This was a trump card that took several tricks, until another expert used a truck loaded with old rails to take the bump. Now, not only did the subtle ones realize that the blowing up of five tons of old iron was a poor result for a half-squadron with their tongues hanging out almost permanently, but also the engine drivers' eyes stuck out as on stalks and became so marvellously penetrating that they could spot a mine, however well hidden, in time to stop the train.

But the most effective of all was the last act. One bright morning the Bolshevik engine driver found himself bumping along the sleepers whilst his wheels were still between the rails. The squadron had opened out the gauge for an inch or so over a length of several hundred yards, spiking the rails neatly down again and covering up their traces.

These experiments in practical railway engineering had cost a certain amount, and all along the line from Ashkhabad to Merv and beyond, the casual traveller saw battered, blackened trucks and coaches lying on their backs by the side of the line, with their wheels in the air. The Russian railway engineers showed wonderful skill and speed in getting things going again after the various crashes and explosions.

At Bairam Ali the Bolsheviks received another blow, and were driven out into the desert between Merv and the Oxus. Towards the end of January 1919 the Bolshevik commander, one Koluzaiev, emboldened by the apparent inactivity of our force, which was really due to orders from home, permitted himself to attack our position, whereupon a well-timed counter-attack drove his troops back in disorder and gained a good deal of ground. However, the order which forbade our troops to follow him up to the Oxus saved him, and a static warfare set in.

During this period an interesting cavalry skirmish took place. A patrol of fourteen Punjabis of the 28th Light Cavalry, working out in the desert, coming over the brow of a sand hill, encountered a squadron of Bolshevik cavalry in open column. Without pausing to think, their dafadar led them at a gallop straight through the centre of the enemy squadron, breaking all four ranks, killing several men, and scattering the formation in confusion. He himself lost three men missing, owing to their horses having been killed, and these eventually rejoined, the last after months of wandering over half Turkestan.

The lull of February gave us time to look round. We had three Turkoman regiments of horse and a battalion of foot. I had seen a few Tekke Turkoman in Tashkent, where they seemed to inspire much awe amongst the Russians, just as a Pathan does in Calcutta; but here we had them in crowds. All the old stories about their wild raiders, and the terror they drove into the hearts of the Persians came back to my mind, so I looked forward to a close acquaintance with them.

The best of the mounted units was that of Colonel Karaz Sardar, a venerable Turkoman chief whom everyone liked very much, but on the whole all four regiments lacked discipline and training almost entirely. In fact, at the Dushak fight they had lost us a good part of the fruits of victory by rioting away to loot a train instead of pursuing the Bolshevik fugitives.

Another misdemeanour of theirs was slitting the throats of fifty or so Magyar and Austrian deserters who were on their way over to us, in response to the patient and oft-repeated appeals of our intelligence branch. Needless to say, this rather choked off any more would-be deserters, and nettled the officer who worked those particular strings.

The Turkoman were good material at bottom, though no amount of training, discipline, or equipment would bring them up to the level of Pathans or Punjabis. But they were keen and willing, so my NCOs drilled and instructed them, especially in the handling of the Lee-Metford rifles that we had issued to them. The results were really most promising. With training and discipline, they would be far from useless mouths, and as it was they had no hesitation in facing Bolsheviks.

The garb they wear marks them out from all other tribes of Asia. Imagine a Guardsman's bearskin of the largest size, made of black sheep's fleece. This is their headgear, light, comfortable to ride in, warm in winter, and by no means as apt to lodge a surplus population as might be expected. Below this a long flowing robe of heavy red silk reaches down to the ankles. The stately robe is girded into the waist by a long silk scarf, tied several times round, holding an automatic pistol or two, and the universal *pichak* – the gently curved, ivory-hilted dagger in its green shagreen sheath.

The horse fills a very large arc of the Turkoman's horizon, larger than does his lady wife, and with some justice. The horse has been for centuries the weapon and the pivotal point of the Tekke's life. Free-moving, clean-limbed, with the broad forehead and the small velvet muzzle of the aristocrat amongst horses, he at once calls to mind the English thoroughbred. There is an idea in England that the English horse of blood has Arab ancestry, though there is mighty little resemblance between a typical Arab and any Irish or English animal. When one has seen the Turkoman, and recollects the 'Byerly Turk' that the Crusade brought to England, there can be little doubt about the origin of our horses, and that their sire was a Turkoman.

During this period I was lucky enough to become the possessor of a thoroughbred Turkoman mare. During a drunken *rixe* in Merv her previous owner, a 'Wachtmister' of Daghestan Horse, came to a violent end from an overdose of lead. My own squadron-dafadar-major, Ahmad Shah, being a Jehlum man, had an eye for a horse if ever anyone had, and moved in the matter. The upshot was that the Wachtmister bequeathed 'Marushka' to me. Like *Ninon de l'Enclos*, the years had passed her over lightly, nor did her lurid past prevent her from being wholly charming in the present. Her youth had been spent as the mount of a Tekke chieftain, and she had seen a good deal of miscellaneous fighting, or raiding, in this sphere. Shortly before the War, she came into the hands of a Cossack subaltern. During the early years of the War, she saw, in Khorasan, many a skirmish with German emissary and Afghan raider. The subaltern left his bones on the scene of his fights, the revolution broke out, and Bicherakov's turbulent but loyal Daghestan Muslims appeared. Marushka, now the long-tailed comrade of the Daghestan Wachtmister, saw many kaleidoscopic changes of fortune. Red revolutions, White counter-revolutions, comic-opera legislative assemblies; all these passed over her well-bred head, and left her unperturbed, if somewhat hungry at times.

The wayward old lady had never been trained, but, on the other hand, she was a living proof of the fact that training is only needed for low-bred animals. A perfect ride, she leaped like a deer, and would scramble up rocky hillsides, covered with sheet ice, in a way that would make the Alpine Club lift their eyebrows. She had a real eye for a country, and was so inured to war that, whilst a mounted man appearing on the skyline left her unmoved if he were unarmed, yet if he had a rifle in his hand she would prick her ears and gently intimate the fact to her rider.

Besides our Turkoman friends, whom we got to like very much, especially their stately grey-bearded chiefs, we saw a good deal of the Russians. The bulk of them were ex-officers and NCOs of the Imperial Army, and an excellent lot. When one thinks of the hardships and never ceasing struggles of some of the Cossack armies, such as that of Orenburg, one cannot but admire the grit and pluck that bids them hold on. Starved of all necessities during the Great War by the canker of a traitorous administration, they endured very much what our wretched people went through in Mesopotamia. Then, betrayed by the Red revolution, they were surrounded on all sides, islets of loyalty to their Crown, in a sea of treachery, and fought almost hopelessly, cut off even from half-hearted Allied aid against the overwhelming swarms of Reds.

Some old officers of this type were with us; in fact with Turkoman aid they manned nearly all the artillery. When their time came they died like gentlemen.

After the last fight, in which the Reds were driven back nearly to Repetek, the fighting was limited to an occasional mild shelling by the armoured trains, or the dropping, now and then, of a home-made bomb from a Bolshevik aeroplane.

It was the first time during the War that I had lived at a headquarters, and I confess that I did not despise the luxury, especially as it helped me over some trouble that I had been having during the winter, in about the twelfth vertebra, the result of too close an acquaintance with a 5.9-inch shell in its business hours, in the old German trench by Neuve Chapelle.

We were entirely dependent on the Russians for our food, and did not do so badly on the fat sheep of the country, though the British Tommies in Ashkhabad groused at getting too much caviar ('That 'ere fish jam, sir!'). We did not, but fresh caviar is rather uninteresting without butter, so we cast about to get some. At last, some twelve miles south of Bairam Ali, towards the Afghan frontier, we found the remarkable phenomenon of a German village. This Lutheran colony had been planted two or three decades ago and made itself quite at home. Both men and women were far from being unfriendly; indeed, they always had some coffee to offer us whilst we sat and listened to their guttural tales of oppression by roving Turkoman, and provided excellent fresh butter for Ashkhabadski rouble notes.

We were pretty comfortable in the Tsar's summer palace, surrounded by a big garden, especially as there was a big bath lined with tiles let into the floor, and a great wood-heated boiler to fill it from. The men played hockey now and then, the gunners of the 44th Battery organized some mounted sports, and we made trips to Merv and the ruins around. For Merv was the 'Queen of the World' in her spacious days of youth, and around the Merv of today there lie the battlemented ruins of four or five great ancient cities built by Macedonian and Mongol, Turk, Tartar, and Arab.

In February 1919 British occupation of the Caucasus began to consolidate itself and our communications with Baku were established. From here ordnance stores and excellent clothing began to find their way to the troops, who were in sore need of them. In March rumours supplemented the material arrivals, and everyone was agog with guessing what was going to happen next. The more ardent spirits hoped for permission to go on to Tashkent, and to smash the Red power in Turkestan for good and all.

Our force stood astride the Central Asian Railway between Merv and Bokhara exercising an influence on events far in excess of its numbers. Stalky Dunsterville had re-captured Baku; the

White Russians seemed in the ascendant – Yudenitch near Petrograd, Kolchak in the Urals, Denikin in Oriol; motorboats of the Royal Navy had torpedoed Russian battle cruisers at Kronstadt; the Soviet forces in Tashkent were cut off from Moscow by the Semirechian Cossacks; the Bokharan ambassador in our camp looked to us for liberation.

So as we studied the situation from the summer palace of the Tsars it seemed as if this could be another of those turning points of history. We knew it needed only a properly conducted push, as Winston put it so succinctly, to 'strangle Bolshevism in its cradle' – at least, for our part, in Turkestan and Transcaspia.

There were four of us; our commander, Brigadier General Beatty, Brigade Major Morris of the 30th Lancers, Staff Captain Ibbetson from Kenya, and myself. To us the stage seemed set for great things.

Suddenly, a despatch rider galloped up with a code signal. It took only a moment to decode it. It was an order to hand over to an Armenian force under a General Lazarev and for ourselves to march south into Persian Khorasan. We were stunned.

Soon the shock and its mists cleared off. 'Would you like me, Sir, to make a slight error in the decoding of this cable?' I asked.

A County Wexford glint lit up our leader's eye. Did he remember Nelson? I hammered away at the hot iron. One good push and we could smash the crumbling Red power in Turkestan, get to Tashkent, and save our loyal and staunch allies. The Russian colonists there were desperate to be liberated by us. In reaching Tashkent we could also safeguard those millions of God-fearing Moslems from the bloody atheisms of Red conquests, massacres and dominations.

Almost on our Commander's lips was his order for the trumpeter to sound 'Boot and saddle', when a British field artilleryman came in with a message for the Staff Captain. It appeared that the British ranks clamoured for their rations to include plum jam, or possibly even raspberry. The spell was broken.

'No, my boy,' said our leader. 'This is not the middle-ages; we must obey orders.'

And that was that.

To our shame, be it said, we were to abandon our Turkoman

allies, and to withdraw into Persia. A counter-revolution which was brought off in Tashkent by one of the many secret societies we had known, under one Osipov, came to nothing, and the resulting Red reprisals cost a great number of lives.

Notes:

The order to withdraw came as a result of a report by General Milne to the War Office in January 1919. He asserted that the capture of Orenburg by the Bolsheviks in December 1918 would allow Bolshevik reinforcements to Turkestan, and concluded: 'We should either assume the burden of complete control and of support, involving time, money and labour in an almost hopeless task, or we should leave the country to its fate with the accompanying anarchy and bloodshed.' On 15 February the order was issued for the withdrawal of General Malleson's force.

Blacker, and many others, felt this decision was pusillanimous. As he points out, the Semirechian Cossacks were still blocking the railway, so despite the fall of Orenburg, Tashkent was still cut off from Orenburg and Moscow. Malleson was in favour of further advance, having already battled his way 200 miles beyond Merv, half way to Bokhara. To take possession of the entire railway from Krasnovodsk to Tashkent would have been a relatively simple matter. Everyone in Tashkent was expecting the British to arrive at any moment, and some of the commissars were preparing their escape. Bailey (who remained in Tashkent for a year after Blacker left in September 1918) felt that only a small British force could have taken the city.

In any event, the War Office took the advice of General Milne. The withdrawal of the 950 men of the British force was completed in April 1919. The Mission retreated into Persia, where it stayed for another year.

It is not certain whether Blacker knew what happened to the huge quantities of baled cotton (see p68):

In Krasnovodsk on 12 July 1918, four months before the end of fighting on the Western Front, several shipments of cotton were being loaded onto ships by German operatives when a certain Captain Teague-Jones arrived on the scene. He immediately grasped the gravity of the situation and made contact with a friendly local named Semov. Thinking fast, they came up with a plan to bribe the Krasnovodsk radio operator. Teague-Jones gave Semov all the money he could spare, and Semov rushed off to see the radio-operator, to whom he told his plan. Shortly thereafter, a message came through to the Soviet Executive Committee to cease loading the cotton and to offload any that had already been loaded. Then the radio station broke down.

Neither the Soviet nor the Germans suspected a thing. The cotton was unloaded and, as things turned out, no more was loaded again – at least not during those two years. None of it ever got to Germany.

Chapter 15

BOKHARA AND AWAL NUR

Before the black day dawned an episode commenced that was no whit behind some of the almost legendary lone-handed exploits of Guides of past generations. The hero was Awal Nur, nobly backed by Kalbi.

Bokhara was a great country, the size of Belgium, rich from commerce and the wealthy corn-lands watered by the Zarafshan River, 'the gold scatterer'. But Bokhara was unable to defend itself against the Red armies, which had free passage along the railway that traverses the middle of the State, and every town teemed with Soviet spies.

Its ruler, the Emir, bore no love for the Bolsheviks. In February 1918 Kolesov let hell loose in the streets of the capital with his armoured cars, so that the alleys ran with blood. This time the Bokharans drove him out, but the Red danger remained.

When the British forces became the allies of the Turkoman, the making of common cause with Bokhara was a natural and foregone conclusion. The Emir asked our General for arms and assistance, and was promised a full measure. The task of seeing the cargo to Bokhara, I entrusted to Awal Nur.

Awal Nur, with whom I had served in five campaigns, had a brilliant war record, having served on the frontier, the better part of a year in East Africa, and the murderous ordeal of half a dozen Flanders battles where he had been wounded three times. The task before him was an immense one, but none better could have been chosen for it than this slim, unassuming youth, a boy in years, but a veteran in wars.

Six hundred miles of awesome desert lay between him and his

goal, and the Soviet lines and their patrols barred the way. It was no mere matter of a few men slipping through; this secret cargo of weapons and ammunition was carried on 100 great Bactrian camels.

Late one night the caravan assembled in the desert outside Merv, and as I said goodbye to the lad I had not much hope of seeing him again alive.

The tale of the outward journey alone forms an epic in itself: waterless marches over innumerable sand dunes that stretched to the horizon all around. Several times the trail was lost, and desperate searches made to find it, or else to find some tiny saxaul bush that marked the way to a foul well of salt and bitter water.

When it came to passing the enemy's outposts, there was no possibility of falling upon the Red picquet and exterminating it, as that would have alerted the commissars. One awful march stretched out its anxious length to ninety-two waterless miles, as they made a huge detour around the well watched by the Red post. Only a happy chance guided them, their tongues black and swollen with thirst, to the next foetid well.

They were glad enough, after many days, to reach the green line that marked the bank of the Oxus, even though, as they clambered up on the far bank, the challenge of a Red patrol rang out. Awal Nur answered with shots, and in a little time the way was cleared, the enemy leaving his dead on the ground.

Another purgatory of parched sandy desert remained to be crossed before the weary, tattered band staggered into Bokhara, their charge intact. The Emir was delighted with his new arrivals, decorating Awal Nur and Kalbi with the Star of Bokhara, and making Awal Nur a Colonel in his army.

This was October of 1919, and their paths now crossed with that of Major Bailey, who had stayed behind in Tashkent back in September 1918. Spies had brought the news to the Tashkent Soviet of a 'British Colonel' in Bokhara. Bailey, hiding from the Reds in Tashkent, disguised himself as a Serbian officer of the Austrian Army and obtained service in the Bolshevik secret service. He was sent to Bokhara to track down this British Colonel, who proved to be none other than his former fellow-soldier Awal Nur.

At length, Awal Nur, Kalbi and Bailey set out again from

Bokhara for a fearsome camel journey to the British lines in Persia, and after a journey no less arduous than the outward passage, they finally arrived safe and sound back at our force headquarters in Meshed.

Chapter 16

KELAT-I-NADIRI

We had a few days in which to observe Denikin's Caucasian troops who were going to relieve us. The more senior officers were a good handful, who had won their spurs against German and Austrian, and if somewhat over-decorated, they had a real pride in their profession of arms and a hatred of the Reds. The Staff rather surprised us by enquiring whether we found it necessary to beat our men very often. This opened our eyes to the class of troops we were dealing with. When we actually saw the regiments and battalions, from a little distance they seemed none so bad. But when one looked into their faces, there was the hang-dog look of vice, the cringe of the fawning slave, and the eye of the slum-bred, scrounging parasite. What a contrast to the straight-backed chivalrous Punjabis, whose hand was never lifted against a weakling, and whose keen eyes looked you straight in the face. It was clear that the riff-raff of Armenia and the Near East had no intention of dying for their own or for anyone else's country.

We packed ourselves into trains to Ashkhabad, the cavalry marched south to Meshed by the shortcut that we had explored in January through the Kara Dagh, and the gunners, with their great American mules, went back to their ship to cross the sea from Krasnovodsk.

I had not been in Ashkhabad before, and there was much of interest to see in the couple of days we spent there. Notably in the cathedral square were four brass guns with King George IV's cipher on them. This made us think a little, until we remembered that the Russians had taken a number of guns from the Afghans at Panjdeh in 1885 that we previously had given them, and here they were, trophies of war in Turkestan. Doubtless the uncivilized young *mujik* recruits of the Turkestan Rifles used to be told that they were captured from the British in the Crimea.

Then we marched out along the fair broad metalled road, gradually ascending over pleasant rolling grass country from which we looked back down on to Ashkhabad, the city that meant so much, and that had cost us such pains to attain.

At Kurd Su, we climbed up, past another little Christian village, then to a crenellated granite fortalice, and so over a barren ridge down into Persia again. As I rode down towards the little huddled village of Bajgiran, I little dreamed that I was going to have to spend a winter and a summer there, looking down to an enemy post. Someone has said that a good deal of the War consisted in going to a little village that you had never heard of before, and never forgetting it all the days of your life.

We marched on to Kuchan in pouring rain over slippery mud in company with a wing of our very good friends, the 19th Punjabis. Kuchan is a pleasant little town lying in the middle of the open valley of the Atrak, that flows from there into the Caspian, flanked by grassy downland of charming aspect under its spring coat of green. Overlooking the town is the tall mound of Alp Arslan, marking the site of one of the Emperor Nadir's pyramids of 10,000 heads and also of his own bloody end.

At Kuchan we met the beginnings of a new corps, the Kurdish Mounted Levy. Like the South Down Militia, 'the terror of the land,' they were going to prove very useful to us later on. The Kurd is an interesting individual; he not only is an Aryan, but, like the Pathan, belongs to the Nordic branch of that race, and his language contains many words that are surprisingly like English. He takes a lot of opium and is on the whole a degenerate being, but retains enough manhood to lick fifty Persians. The Kurds behaved well in our service, and filled a gap better than anyone else could have done, and when a difficult time came later on, they showed an admirable loyalty to us.

Some ninety miles of marching along a level alluvial valley took us to Meshed, where the force concentrated.

During April all was quiet, and our situation seemed secure enough, at any rate for a few months. Kolchak, Yudenitch, and

Denikin were doing well, and there seemed no reason why General Lazarev's army should not only hold the Merv front that we had handed over to him, and even go on to monarchist Bokhara. So we had a short breathing space between wars, and time to look around us.

There was an eminently seeable sight three marches north of Meshed, Kelat-i-Nadiri, a mysterious and very secret stronghold established by the famous emperor Nadirshap. The Force Commander General George F. Milne, who succeeded Beatty, decided to pay a visit to this place, and took me with him and a small escort. We set out on a sunny morning in April, and marched for three days through a succession of ever more astonishing natural phenomena. As we rode out of a strange gorge known as the Gully of the Unbeliever, there sprang into our view a straight-crested tooth line of stark cliffs. This was the thousand-foot rampart of the Kelat itself. This sheer cliff wall ran for several miles to the north-west and the south-east in a line as straight as an arrow, as if planned by a draughtsman. The green fold spurs and valleys of the natural run of the country it seemed to ignore, and one could imagine them surging like wintry breakers against a sea-wall about its flanks. Here and there a watch tower, outlining itself against the sky, showed the hand of man.

We spent the night as guests of the Khan, whose hospitality, and that of his followers, lacked for nothing. The next morning we climbed up the reddish slopes that form part of the northern wall of the fortress. From there we could look down for immense distances on to the boundless plain that sweeps northwards to the very coasts of the Arctic Ocean. To our right we could see the tiny black spot in the desert that marked the oasis of Dushak, where the 19th Punjabis had fought their hardest battle; to the north in the dim distance another such marked the village of Artik, where Punjabi blood was first shed in the country of the Turkoman. Straight in front of us, it seemed almost at our feet; little puffs of smoke showed us where the armoured trains of loyalists and Bolsheviks were locked in their conflict. Only later were we to realize what tragedies were being played out before our eyes.

Chapter 17

THE THIRD AFGHAN WAR

Even as I stood on the peak of the Kelat, sketch-block in hand, a Scotch mist came down over the mountains, shutting out the view, and it was followed by a hearty downpour.

Next day the sky poured down in torrents and, as the mist swirled round the peaks, we kept to the inside of the Khan's palace, enjoying his hospitality and his old-time legends. That Turkish coffee is something one remembers for many years. For two days more the deluge continued. The mountain streams outside flowed into impassable torrents, whilst the clay of the valleys became as slippery as ice. Our explorations were brought to a sudden end by an insistent and rather startling message from the staff at Meshed that told us we were plunged into still another war.

In February 1919 young Amanullah succeeded to the throne of Kabul, and had decided to cut his milk teeth on the Government of India.

The situation was curious from our own point of view, since our tiny force of only one Regular battalion, one regiment of cavalry, and two somewhat ramshackle levy corps, was confronted by a whole Afghan division, scarcely ten easy level marches from us, complete with a brigade of cavalry, a machine-gun company, several batteries of breech-loading guns, and a Bolshevik alliance. It was the Soviet, needless to say, who had organized the Third Afghan War.

As far as the troops were concerned, it was even possible that we should have had to retire westwards over the immense tract that separated us from our force in North-West Persia.

112

This would certainly have been the case had the Reds taken Merv sooner in order to join hands with the Afghans, and if the wily and volatile Afghan tribesmen had scratched up any enthusiasm for their ruler Amanullah's little war. Luckily for us, they did not. The bold Afghan may be a first-class fighting man, but not when he happens to be a Regular soldier.

However my NCOs again occupied the place of honour on the actual Afghan frontier and in close contact with the Afghan outpost troops. This lasted for several weary months and in the meantime the rest of my detachment was employed all over Northern Khorasan mapping the wild rocky valleys, in many of which no surveyor had yet set foot.

Small patrols of my men came often into contact with Afghan outposts, and one way or another, several excellent little horses came into our hands. Anyone who knows the Afghan will realize how very early in the morning one must rise in order to prize away anything from him, above all a horse.

By the end of May Amanullah's men had been driven decisively out of the few Indian towns they had occupied, so the Third Afghan War gradually subsided, and we lost interest in it. It became quite clear that the Herat Division of the Afghan army were not going to attack us.

So we made our way back to Meshed in June 1919, making a short excursion en route to visit the tomb of Omar Khayyam. When we got to Meshed there was a corpse dangling from the tall gallows in front of our villa billet. This was some poor wretch who had not enough money to escape the exactions of the Persian police.

The 19th Punjabis, after their five solid years of tough campaigning in the awful deserts of Khorasan, were now being relieved by an Indian regiment of the Hyderabad contingent. So my lads invited them to a smoking concert to celebrate their departure home. A gargantuan repast, music and revelry organized by Aslam, and a revue which included a scurrilous and wholly insubordinate imitation of the revered Adjutant, lasted to the early hours of the morning. Then we turned in a couple of hours sleep before seeing them off for the start of their 700-mile return home.

The countryside was only roughly mapped, much was frankly

labelled 'unexplored', and the rest but nebulously sketched in piecemeal by various travellers. Practically all the pioneer mapping of Northern and Eastern Persia had been done by men of the Guides. Hence it was up to us to fare far afield, to reconnoitre routes, and to make sketches in view of what the future might hold for us.

Note:

The British had long dreaded an invasion of India from Afghanistan. On 4 May 1919 Afghan forces, numbering 50,000, did invade. But British and Indian forces responded in strength and by the end of the month King Amanullah was forced to sue for peace.

Blacker's contribution was greater than he admits to in his memoir. Moscow initially supported the Afghans, but after a campaign of deception orchestrated by General Malleson, the Russians became convinced that Amanullah wanted to attack *them* and withdrew their support. Malleson mentions Blacker as one of his two 'excellent officers, speaking numerous languages' who spread mistrust between the two sides (the other was Ernest Redl).

Chapter 18

WINTER IN BAJGIRAN

Just two months later, thanks to the treachery of the large Armenian element amongst them, the Volunteer army of General Lazarev, which had taken over from us in April 1919, lost Annenkoff and Merv that the 19th Punjabis had so dearly won.

Many of the Imperial officers that we had known died like gentlemen, and the survivors, pitiably weak in numbers, marched back westwards towards the sea. Every now and then the Reds, having repaired with slave labour the line that the Whites blew up behind them, would overwhelm them on both flanks. It was an episode of this phase that the Colonel and I had watched from the crest of the dizzy rampart of Kelat-i-Nadiri.

They made a last stand at Bala Ishem, in the desert. From this very few of our old acquaintances escaped alive; guns, trains, and aircraft were lost, and in a few days the Reds had occupied Krasnovodsk on the Caspian Sea. A trainload of sailors, searchlights, and naval guns was soon on its way to establish coastal defences there.

The enemy, after massacring the leaders of the Menshevik party in the Ashkhabad administration had every intention of making an inroad into Khorasan. Whilst they were utterly incapable of meeting our Regular infantry, however much the odds in their favour, they were overwhelmingly superior in modern war material, of which indeed we had none at all, unless one reckons as modern, four mountain guns designed in the eighties of the last century. It is an ill business pitting bare flesh and blood, however staunch, against chrome-steel plates and TNT.

The Bolshevik advance had laid bare the head of the only road

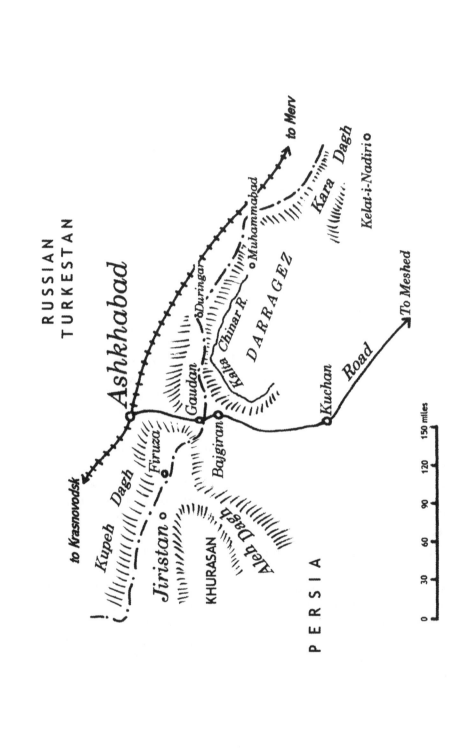

practicable for wheeled traffic that leads from Turkestan into Persia. Now they were no longer restricted to camel tracks, bridle paths and steep hills which their vice-sodden infantry flatly refused to climb. They could put their troops from their foetid armoured trains into lorries, bring their numerous armoured cars and their overwhelming artillery into action against us, and cover all with their aeroplanes. The frontier had to be watched, not only to give warning to our commander of a regular attack, but also to keep out spies and propagandists.

I received orders to take my little following to Bajgiran to watch 160 miles of rugged mountain frontier, to gather information, and to prevent Bolshevik penetration into Persia.

Feroz and I were whisked off by our General to the Persian post of Bajgiran, where I found a company of Indian infantry under Captain Duncan, a platoon of Mongol Hazara levies, and a handful of Kurd jigits, paid, armed, and clothed by us.

Every day crowds of deserters of every nationality came to us, escaping from the Red Army and the Red Terror. We were bound by the custom of the Service to feed and clothe them, whether friendly or hostile, and were glad to do it. A great number of hard cases turned up, mostly ex-soldiers from strange parts of the old Russian Empire.

One such was Ivan Petruski Skivar, who resided at Kalta Chinar, a rough morning's scramble to the east. He was a volcanic Georgian by birth, of good family, and born in Ashkhabad, where his father had been a high military officer. As a Captain on the Galician front, he had been very severely wounded in 1916. He became, by way of 'light duty', the Commander of a frontier guard squadron on this border, where in his boyhood he knew all the local Tekkes and their chiefs. In the revolution his brother was barbarously murdered by a Jew commissar, and Ivan stepped over the frontier and lived with a friend of his, a Tekke chief.

When I came into Bajgiran, Ivan had just ridden in from Kalta Chinar with a bullet wound in his arm, a saddlebag full of recently won 'souvenirs', a brand-new Russian rifle and pistol, and a complacent look on his visage, as one who should say: 'I may have a bit of a hole in my arm, but you should just see the other fellow.' The other fellow, it transpired, had been a petty

Armenian commissar, in charge of the Bolshevik post at Russian Kalta Chinar, who was now, with his cronies, running back into Turkestan, bloody and out of breath, minus three ponies, some weapons, and other properties that they had not leisure to remove. It made a rather tricky situation, as we had very stringent orders to avoid affrays with the Reds, but fortunately the Armenian commissar concealed the scuffle from the Soviet, and so the whole thing blew over, except that our side retained the swag. Ivan Petruski Skivar, who was clearly a personality and a moving force, came into our services, and in a few days had established himself in the esteem of all my men.

The refugees were destined to become an increasingly difficult problem. Straight away I found that most of them were destitute, if not actually starving. They had to be escorted to Kuchan, or else bandits who waited along the road would take them and sell the women as slaves. It was a four-day journey and the poor creatures usually had nothing of their own, so the kind-hearted sepoys used to give a portion of their own meagre rations to hungry Russian and Polish women and children. This seemed hard on my men: by insisting on them moving under a guard, we had assumed responsibility for the refugees, and so for feeding them. Soon I managed to get sanction for a limited issue of rations.

When the winter began to close in, and the stark hillsides became covered with snow, the half-naked escapers suffered very much from lack of clothing. They came from a plain 4,000 feet lower down into a climate that got more rigorous each day. Again I had to use my best bureaucratic eloquence to get a small allowance of inconceivably inferior clothing for bona fide soldiers, but not before they went through some terrible hardships from blizzards and frost-bite.

The many scores that passed through my hands behaved very well indeed, if one excepts the fawning of one or two town-bred civilians.

Perhaps the most trying case was that of a young pair of Bohemians, man and wife. My interrogations and discreet enquiries showed that Mr Bohemian had remained in Russia in 1914 to dodge the Austrian conscription, and took some pride in the fact. I asked him what Russian regiment he had honoured by joining, and was answered by a blank stare. Needless to say, he had shirked Russian service as well, subsiding into a mild sort of civilian internment in Tashkent. Yet he seemed to expect to receive rations and clothes at the expense of the British taxpayer. He was disillusioned, and took it very badly. He funked going back to Bolshevik rule and eventually scrounged his way to Meshed, and Heaven knows what happened to them there. It flabbergasted me to think that, having shirked everything in the War and betrayed both sides, he expected to share in one of the few privileges a soldier has.

Of a different type was a quaint trio that suddenly turned up: an old Russian lady – the widow of a Tsarist General, so she said, and she certainly had some unimpeachable references – with her daughter, a very good-looking girl indeed, and her fiancé. He was an Armenian of mawkish aspect, a painter by profession, almost certainly guilty of Cubism and suspected of Dadaism. An unwholesome creature, he wore his yellow hair long on his shoulders, and over it he wore a quilted cap with a flap, day and night. My intelligence bureau informed me that he had been a sanitary official of sorts under the Ashkhabad Soviet, adding that seven million roubles missing from their funds would probably be found sewn into the quilted tea-cosy-like headgear. Ivan Petruski warmly advocated shooting him and running through the tea-cosy, adding that a beauteous damsel like that was wasted on an Armenian, and that it made him sick to watch her making eyes at the wretch all day long. I could not acquiesce in his plan; besides, an armful of Soviet roubles was worth nothing in any case.

A day or two later there turned up a very decent pair of Austrian officers, one of whom was a Tyroler of an Alpine regiment with an Edelweiss on his collar badges, the other a sapper. We brought them in to tea and they told us of their adventures. Casually, I asked the sapper if he had heard anything of the old lady, her daughter, and the Armenian in Ashkhabad. 'Oh yes,' he replied briskly; 'why, I married that girl myself only a few days ago.' Loud laughter ensued from the cheaper parts of the house, as he explained that a woman would assume Austrian nationality by marrying an Austrian officer, assisting her to get out of Soviet clutches into Persia.

The front of 160 miles that had to be patrolled by my handful of men, much wider than the British front in France and incomparably rougher, was maintained month in and month out. It was an unceasing watch for the three most important miles, nearest the road that tempted the Red General Staff. The remainder of the 160 miles for which I was responsible were patrolled by a handful of my Guides. I could use but a bare dozen for this duty, and so fifty-six sheepskin-bonneted tribesmen, with their tribal chiefs, enlisted into the Kurdish Mounted Levy and were placed under my orders.

By December the winter had closed in: a deep snow, which made the road impassable for wagons, cut us off from our support fifty miles back at Kuchan. In these months blizzards were constant, the whole countryside lay under snow, immense drifts blocked the passes, and sheet ice made a nightmare of the precipitous slopes.

The men, in spite of hardships and privations, were wonderful. My imperturbable havildars, youthful veterans of seven campaigns, would turn out at a moment's notice at midnight into a snowstorm, to lead a patrol of Kurds into some unexplored valley upon a perilous quest.

The line, its right-hand post on a craggy peak, looked down upon the tiny Russian village of Gaudan, the Russian customs post, thousands of feet below. Its central group, the examining post on the road, was but a musket-shot from the castellated granite fort that in Imperial times had held a troop of Cossacks in its clean little whitewashed barrack, with glazed windows and smartly painted doors. Now an insanitary gang of Red Guards lounged about, spat on the floors, and broke the windows in their drunken orgies.

But the Bolsheviks had a plan. Seldom did a week pass without one of my trusty henchmen bringing in a neat packet of, say, 500 scarlet leaflets, or a couple of dozen Marxian pamphlets, with the imprimatur of the Ashkhabad Soviet. Accompanying these would be a beaky Armenian or astrakhan-capped Tabrizi Turk in many-pleated frockcoat, as greasy and unwashed as they make them, with an NCO's heel rope round his neck. As matters developed their propaganda took a pronounced anti-British turn, appealing to the oppressed multitudes to shake off their 'capitalistic imperialistic' oppressors.

One of the more interesting things that the Transcaspian commissars pushed into Persia was a 5-foot lithographed poster, depicting in several colours three naked, emaciated Dravidians harnessed into a plough at the tail of which stood a ginger-whiskered John Bull, in white drill jacket and sun helmet, complete with projecting incisors and bulldog pipe. In one hand he brandished an automatic pistol, in the other a *nagaïka*, and the legend told one 'this is how the English plough in India'.

Even the Turkoman, who had rubbed shoulders with our Punjabis, laughed derisively when they saw this, and it was far too clumsy to take in the nimble-willed Persian.

I think it was Wassmuss, a thorn in our side, who conceived the idea of having several hundred copies of the Verestchagin painting circulated for Persian consumption. Verestchagin painted a most vivid picture of the punishment of the ringleaders of the Akali rebellion of 1877. In the painting, a battery of 9-pounders is formed up as in action, the white-robed fanatics lashed to their muzzles, and the British artillerymen standing to attention, lanyard, rammer, sponge, and handspike in fists, whilst a white-helmeted, gold-laced gunner Captain looks at a stop-watch. The vivid realism of Verestchagin, the glaring light of the picture, and the full-dress uniforms make it a very striking scene.

The idea was to show the simple Persian what brutal blood-stained hooligans the British were. But it had a different effect. The Persian saw it and reflected, 'Bismillah, and by Gum! we always thought that the English were a cheery, easy-going sort of crowd, but if they really go in for this sort of frightfulness, and Wassmuss says they do, we had better not thwart them.'

Their productions, however, soon became more subtle, and the bureaus and railway trains, for their dissemination developed into a remarkable institution. By the spring they had half a dozen such trains moving slowly about the railways of Turkestan, from town to town. Each train carried a printing machine for leaflets and brochures, a litho press for posters, a communist library, a cinema with a selection of Bolshevik films, and a staff of lecturers. It was said that some of the trains had bathrooms, but we did not believe that. The modus operandi was to halt at a town, collect all available inhabitants, and treat them to the train's whole repertoire, machine guns being provided to ensure a good box-office and to respond to hecklers.

One bright May morning a deputation of Turkoman patriarchs from Duringar and Kalta Chinar waited on me, and informed me of the activities of one Oraz Mahomed.

Oraz was connected with a certain news writer at Muhammadabad named Mursal. Mursal interviewed many of the Russian refugees who, with a few hardly-saved jewels or trinkets, came his way, and with suave, courteous phrases speeded them towards Meshed and the British lines. A swift message would go out to Oraz, a few of whose scoundrels would then rob the wretched party in the first lone mountain defile they reached. Mursal deplored these occurrences on paper whilst in fact dividing the booty with Oraz, and also with the Governor of Darragez.

Oraz, with the approval of the Governor, had usurped the title of Deputy Governor of Duringar and dispossessed the hereditary Kurdish Beg of the village, who was a friend of ours. Then, not content with collecting rents from all the hamlets in the Darragez valley, whether Kurd or Turkoman, he robbed and blackmailed as well. He was of a truculent disposition, went about with a loaded Mauser pistol slung well to the front, and kept a gang of gunmen with magazine rifles.

That he was now Deputy Governor made the situation more delicate: a trial of strength was on the carpet between the Governor of Darragez and British prestige.

I comforted the old gentlemen of the deputation, and wired to headquarters so that a reprimand might be administered to Oraz by the Governor General.

Oraz did not let the Governor General's admonitions keep him awake. Perhaps he thought that I was some callow subaltern instead of being a sour and cynical Field Officer. Things got no better – they got worse in fact. The Kurd levies of our standing patrol intimated that Oraz Mahomed's pin-pricks were being directed against them, and we heard that flirtations were going on between him and the Bolsheviks. A column of poor journalese which appeared in the Ashkhabad newspaper *Sovietski Turkestan* describing how a certain capitalistic, imperialistic, *angliski* officer named 'Blakker,' assisted by a vile Georgian counter-revolutionary, was oppressing the innocent inhabitants of the Kurd country.

Matters were made difficult for me by the fact that Duringar was too far for me to visit without being several days away from my headquarters and getting out of touch with Red Army activities in Ashkhabad. Also I was expressly forbidden to meddle with internal Persian affairs.

Then one day young Ali Akbar came in from a patrol and informed us that Oraz Mahomed had lifted a cow from a cousin of his. As if this were not enough, one of Ivan Petruski Skivar's Turkoman cronies rode in from Kalta Chinar to announce that Oraz had made away with an excellent pair of boots belonging to him: Russian sapagees, no less. I thought of *Who dares this pair of boots displace, Must meet Bombastes face to face*, but I dared not smile when Ivan Petruski was about.

Now, Ivan and Ali Akbar were an officer and a man directly under my command. I could not ignore Oraz's attack upon them. The matter ceased to be an internal Persian affair, but a personal one between him and me. I determined to ride over, scotch the snake for better or worse, and stand or fall by the upshot of it. I expected nothing less than a court-martial if I went beyond my orders: I could expect nothing but the total failure of my work if I did not keep up my prestige in Duringar.

Ivan Petruski, Aslam and Abdullah Shah had long held the theory that I should be an absolute dictator in the south-east Caspian frontier region, pistolling at sight anyone who thwarted my plans. This, however, was hardly the idea that my military superiors held of my job, still less the Politicals, so I was forced to moderate his enthusiasm.

A dozen of us rode out one fine day over the great mountain of Baba Asalmeh to Kalta Chinar.

All around, the towering bulk of the mountain is buttressed by precipices and sliced abruptly off by perpendicular scarps, from the brink of which we looked down into the fair valley and slender white poplars of Duringar. Suddenly, 100 yards ahead the two Kurds of our 'point' dismounted like a streak and exchanged a dozen rapid snap-shots with some ruffians on the opposite spur.

For these occasions I devised a way of counterbalancing the slowness of an automatic pistol in comparison with a revolver in getting off its first shot. I used to charge up the magazine of my .450 Colt, then put an extra (eighth) round into the chamber. This left the hammer at full cock, but instead of applying the safety catch, which means fumbling and delay at a critical moment, I let it carefully down to half-cock, replaced the magazine, and kept the safety catch in the 'fire' position. I could then let off the first round quicker than with a revolver, and fire eight aimed shots even at a gallop, in less time than one could discharge the six chambers of a Webley.

So the bandits scuttled away over the crest-line, and we rode on.

After a steep scramble down about 5,000 feet we rode into the pleasant glen and then into the larger valley of Kalta Chinar. We stayed under the roof-tree of a patriarchal Turkoman, a friend of Skivar's, where we listened to the lurid details of the rape of the boots. The horses had a splendid time in a lucerne patch, and next morning we trotted up the charming little green valley, between the rough stone walls of little fields and vineyards, to Duringar. Sure enough outside the village was Oraz waiting for us, with his fist on his Mauser and his bravos behind him.

To his great surprise, I cut him dead, and so did everyone. He was baffled beyond words. We rode on past him into the house of our friend Mahomed Beg, the rightful chief.

Inside over a cup of tea and a cigarette, Mahomed Beg and his old father acquainted us with the latest developments, whilst odd Kurds and small boys popped in every few minutes to tell us how Oraz was looking.

Ivan Petruski still continued to urge me to shoot him and get it over, but mindful of that general court martial hanging over my head, I thought of a better plan.

At the corner of the village was the corporal's guard that were supposed to attend to law and order in the valley. I sent for the under-sized, sallow, knock-kneed corporal, who came into the Beg's room and saluted with his hand to his grubby sheepskin cap. He seemed a little overpowered, not to say bewildered, when I explained that I had a complaint to prefer against an individual named Oraz Mahomed, in the matter of, firstly, a pair of excellent boots; secondly, a cow belonging to ranks under my command; and would he be kind enough to deal with the matter by apprehending the named individual. At this the corporal's knees took on the aspect of a buzzer armature, and he opined that when 'constabulary duty's to be done, to be done, a policeman's life is not a happy one'; in other words, that Oraz and his merry men would certainly shoot him and all his gendarmes at the opening syllable of the word 'arrest'.

'That will be all right,' said I, 'you can call upon my lads to assist you in the execution of your duty.' The lads in question grinned a cheerful assent, but still the corporal displayed symptoms of a strong vertical breeze. Then a tall Kurdish dafadar whispered into his ear what might happen if he failed in his duty.

I gave the little man my charge in writing, and he decided that he had to see it through one way or the other.

It was all over very quickly. The corporal's quick Persian wit came to his assistance in his time of need. He enticed Oraz alone into the gendarmerie yard, the jackbooted tough never thinking that the policeman would dream of arresting him. A dozen volunteers closed in from various dark corners upon the gateway, and Oraz was trapped.

Ivan Petruski Skivar was frankly disgusted at the pacific upshot of the business, but the whole village buzzed with excitement as I walked into the little mud police station to chat with the man. He was pale green with fright and the sudden collapse of his power.

When I asked him who he was, he plucked up courage to say that he was the Deputy Governor of Duringar, and produced a commission to that effect, scrawled on a half-sheet of notepaper, and signed by Zaberdast Khan, the Governor of Darragez.

It was politely explained to him that he might be half a dozen full-blown Governors, yet not be allowed to help himself to my men's footgear or their cousins' cows.

In less than half an hour the now thoroughly deflated tyrant had his ankles lashed under the belly of a sorry nag, his wrists bound behind his back, and was proceeding towards Kalta Chinar.

As luck would have it, an important Bolshevik commissar had chosen that moment to visit, and as we rode past, his following and mine glared at each other over a couple of hundred yards of temptingly level green turf, and fingers itched at triggers. Ivan Petruski looked like an insecurely plugged volcano. Now all the world had seen Oraz Mahomed tied up like a sack of potatoes on an old jade, and his prestige was ruined.

125

As I expected, ready tongues quickly bore the tale to Mursal and Zaberdast Khan, and from them a galloping courier carried an indignant bleat to the Governor General of Khorasan.

True Persian hyperbole described how a domineering, swashbuckling British officer had made an unprovoked onslaught on a bona fide Deputy Governor, a lamblike and innocent official of the State, shooting up the countryside the while.

A telegram from headquarters called upon me for an explanation. In the Army, as 'The Young Officer's Guide to Knowledge' tells us, no one is ever called upon to furnish his reasons in writing unless it is well known that he has none to offer. This, however, was the exception that proves the rule, and my explanation was approved.

During all these months I had carried on with the mapping of the unknown and half-known bits of North Khorasan that lay within a week or ten days' march of us.

I was able myself to go out for a few days at a time on one or two mapping expeditions, but most of the work was done by young and energetic Sardars and NCOs with the minimum of supervision. They all worked extraordinarily hard with the utmost devotion to duty: the work was constantly being interrupted and topographers taken away from mapping to deal with disturbances, and by actual fighting. During the winter the weather conditions were abominable; sleet, snow, and blizzards or constant rain were the mapper's daily lot, and they frequently had to work in quasi-hostile country. The essence of the matter was mobility. As the country was unsettled, each party had to include six rifles. The topographers, assistants, cooks, and escort were all mounted and armed.

During 1919 and early 1920, in spite of the many interruptions, they dealt with nearly 14,000 square miles of country, of which an appreciable proportion was, up till then, not only unsurveyed, but unexplored.

The months we spent at Bajgiran were not all work, nor alarums and excursions. For one thing, the hospitality of the Persian functionaries had to be returned. Especially where Hassan Khan was concerned, the proceedings were anything but dull. Hassan did not spurn that alchemist who transmutes life's leaden metal into gold, and his conviviality was irresistible. Whether it was fiery arrak, or the golden fluid that the Nishapuri vintners squeezed from their grapes, it was all the same to Hassan Khan. To his tongue it brought erudite quotations from Molière and Hafiz, Sa'adi and Shakespeare, mixed with twentieth-century drinking songs in half a dozen tongues.

When he was being taken home in the early hours, he would execute weird and warlike dances in the snow of the main street, until the voice of Mrs Hassan Khan would say from behind her door, in a tone that foretold domestic troubles: 'Hassan Khan, drunk again?'

Ivan Petruski was another element of briskness at these gatherings: Georgian dinner-party etiquette seemed to involve his sitting down bristling with weapons from a Nagant to a Kinjal. There was no great depth to his potations, but his accommodation for them was shallow, so that on one occasion of his becoming warlike, it was only the missing fire of a cap that prevented the untimely demise of an esteemed guest. After that we always made him leave all guns and knives at the door.

Not the least appreciated phase of life in Bajgiran was one for which we were indebted to the Soviets of Turkestan and Transcaspia: I refer to the succession of entertaining, vivacious, and comely Russian damsels that they sent to us for espionage purposes. Surviving commissars concerned will please accept this, the one and only notification of our thanks.

Soon the minor worries and the more pleasant humours of life in Bajgiran were replaced by the clash of arms.

Chapter 19

THE STAG-BEETLE OF GILYAN

Bigger events were moving over the frontier. The Soviets were not idle. The ice of the Volga had melted; destroyers and even submarines, laboriously transported by rail piecemeal from Kronstadt, were taking up positions in the Hyrcan Sea. In February 1920 the Reds took Krasnovodsk, and the poor remains of the Volunteer fleet, bereft of a home port after the fall of Baku, cruised about till their fuel was exhausted, whereupon they subsided into internment in Enzeli port. We heard that some had offered their ships and crews for hire to various seaboard states either for war or commerce. Two ships, I believe, *Kars* and *Australia*, went over to the Bolsheviks, after the customary massacre of officers, whilst the wretched port guardship at Ashurada was taken by boarding.

The Reds were now free to devote their time to their incursion into Persia, a country they intended to use as a jumping-off place for their psychological warfare against British rule in India. The Red Army had the utmost aversion to facing our troops, after its experiences with the 19th Punjabis, but was still torn with a desire to loot the fat valleys of Khorasan. The wool and wheat of fertile Darragez were irresistible in their attraction for the starved, ragged, and verminous Soviet forces. Several times during March, April and May they concentrated troops, aircraft, and artillery at Ashkhabad, and their objective was only too plain. Indeed the Soviet never lost sight of their goal in Persia (which they later reached).

The unstinting and tireless energy of my patrols had made it so unsafe for the enemy's emissaries to cross the frontier that eventually the Soviet could find no one for the job. They had to think of some other way of bringing on the revolution that they yearned for in Persia and India. For diplomatic reasons in Europe they avoided the idea of a simple invasion by troops of the established Red Army.

To this end, the Reds suborned a certain Khuda Verdi Sardar, a petty Kurdish chief, with promises and arms to revolt. He owned a castle by Gilyan in the inaccessible crags of the Aleh Dagh. Before we came on the scene, he had derived a comfortable livelihood from brigandage. The loss of this made him a ready tool to the Reds' hand, and they decided to make the most of him.

Khudu, as we came to know him, strongly resembled a stagbeetle in his personal appearance, and had a certain driving power and ruthlessness. The Reds intended that he should start an insurrection of the Kurds against the Persians. The revolt would be directed against the Persian Government, which was equivalent to calling it an anti-British outbreak. When it developed he would proclaim his self-determination and form a Kurdish republic independent of Persia. Then, as in Azerbaijan, and in many other countries, he would invite the Red army and its Soviets to help him maintain his independence against capitalist imperialism.

This incursion into Persia was the first that the Soviets had planned against any country that had, in the old days, been independent of Russia, and so, for a few months our squalid frontier village became the centre and focus of world politics.

The Communists were smuggling quantities of modern weapons, of which they had no lack, through from Ashkhabad to Khudu's castle. The NCOs who commanded my patrols kept me informed of all these comings and goings, and of the movements of Khudu and his younger brother Allah. But we were not allowed to stop these smugglings by force of arms, since higher authority laid down that it was an internal affair of Persia. No doubt, too, it was politic to give Khudu and the Reds enough rope to hang themselves with.

The situation was delicate, and I had every reason to be grateful to my Pathan Guides for the discipline they displayed. Heaven knows what a mental ordeal it must have been for them to restrain themselves from attacking those cargoes of rifles that they knew were going to be used against themselves before long.

Needless to say, the Persian authorities did nothing to help. Weak, corrupt, and vacillating, they preferred to drift with the tide, and to accept the enemy's bribes rather than run the risk of stopping a Kurdish bullet.

I was less cynical then than I am now. Rumours of an impending British withdrawal from Persia had been current since about March. Every Staff Officer and soldier had preserved the most stringent secrecy in the matter, but a fat-head in the accounts department had sent a long wire in 'clear' dealing with the financial arrangements for the move. Even the Red newspapers touched on the matter; at the end of June the Bolsheviks' preparations were nearly ready and Ashkhabad was full of troops and guns.

Early in July the political atmosphere was electric. The Kurds in their alpine pastures and in their towered loopholed villages were as polite and hospitable as ever to British officers and to my patrols, but we knew that the storm would soon burst. We even knew which tribes would take the field against us.

One fine day 'Christopher Columbus,' our little doctor, and Captain Duncan's subaltern went off to the village of Jiristan, some twenty-two miles to the west of Bajgiran, to pay a visit to the cheery Persian customs man there, to inspect our detachment of Kurds, and to inspect its sanitation (or the Kurdish equivalent for it).

The two officers rode in at about tea-time with a small escort. It quickly became clear that the hilltops all around were being occupied by watchers, rifle in hand. To make matters quite clear, a polite brigand rode in with a note, composed by Khudu himself, in which he gave the subaltern half an hour to clear out of Jiristan and the British twenty-four hours to clear out of Persia.

The subaltern continued his tea with the doctor, without undue haste. After tea he felt that since the morning's ride had been a long one, forty winks would not be amiss. Then he dictated a polite response to Khudu, deploring his inability to comply with the stag-beetle's wishes.

After dark he and the doctor decided to ride back to headquarters, as it had become clear that the gun-running was on a very large scale indeed.

They rode up the valley to the hamlet of Namanlu three miles off, and then between rough slopes that leap sheer up into naked black and yellow cliffs of 10,000 feet. It was pitch dark when a sudden ragged volley blazed out at them. A bullet from a Russian Berdanka glanced off the subaltern's pistol-butt and struck him in the hip; but the Kurds that laid the ambush did not show any desire to close with the little party, so our young subaltern was able to ride back to headquarters with the doctor and to put us abreast of the situation.

By daybreak, the whole countryside had risen up. Every moss-trooper of that rough frontier was to horse on his little shaggy stallion, armed to the teeth, and riding to the standard of his chieftain.

Soon Khudu's men had besieged our little outpost at Jiristan. The post contained only six men, but there were many of our patrols cut off further up the valley. The more distant detachments marched in from their remoter valleys, bluffing and hectoring their way through half-hostile villages. They fought a dozen skirmishes in a few days, and soon all were concentrated at Jiristan.

The houses of this cluster of mud abodes were put into a state of defence by the energy of the war-taught Abdullah Shah. The next day they were joined by more troops of Kurdish levies, and a company of ragged, starved, cur-like Persian infantry. Soon Jiristan was completely cut off by Khudu's forces.

Communication with Jiristan was scrappy and uncertain; occasionally a man could dodge through the Kurdish watchers by night with a message. On the third day of the siege a runner came through by stealth, describing how the Persian infantry had fled in panic when a couple of them had been wounded in a mild attack; he also told us their ammunition was beginning to run dangerously low.

Captain Duncan and I were the only unwounded combatant officers left at Bajgiran, and we, together with the Regular infantry, were strictly forbidden to leave that post, on account of the massing of the Red Army on the road in front of us. It was painfully obvious that the Russians were trying to draw off some of the regular infantry from my main body, and so leave open the road into Khorasan. I then realized the extraordinary loneliness

131

of the commander in the field. Everyone looks to him automatically for orders.

I had altogether six squadrons and companies made up of cavalry and infantry of the Guides, our Kurdish Mounted Levy and our Khorasan Levy Corps. Although it gave the Russians a healthy respect for us, it was not much to play with. It was necessary to make up my mind to relieve Jiristan without at the same time letting them charge up the cart road. So I sent in as large a force as I dared.

That night a patrol of eight levies under Alam Khan, a young Regular NCO, took out a couple of ammunition mules destined for Jiristan. He was a little too rash, tried to bullock his way through, and lost nearly all his men in an ambush. A wounded man rode back with the news of this skirmish, which had not improved the situation at all. Now Alam Khan and his wounded men had to be helped out of the nasty hole they were in.

The insurgents were more cock-a-hoop than ever. Khudu had announced in the bazaars that he had pistolled a British officer with his own hand. Except for the fact that the British officer was still alive and quite hearty, that there was no pistol in the business, and that it was not Khudu who had pressed the trigger, the statement was quite true.

A relieving column was formed. My own Wurdi Major Amal Baz of the Guides Cavalry led the little force. The tiny column fell in in the narrow cobbled main street of Bajgiran village. Its composition was somewhat unconventional. The mounted troops were a couple of sections of sheep-skinned Kurdish levies; next came a squad of Regular bombers, mainly of the Guides; for artillery a single Lewis gun with its team of very youthful Khatak gunners under a boy lance naik; and the main body was a platoon of Hazara foot levies under a wizen-faced Mongol officer.

The senior NCO of the column was Aslam. I well remember the scene when he collected the reports, and how the last rays of the setting sun fell on the furrows made by a Bavarian grenade that ploughed his cheek at Loos. Aslam had been thrice severely wounded in France, Belgium, and Africa, once indeed desperately, yet never lost his ardour for any new affray, even after seven years of fighting.

A few miles brought them into the mouth of the valley and in touch with the enemy. A rattle of fire broke out. In moments the column was engaged, and the enemy were soon driven off. Here they picked up the wounded of the first patrol and sent them home. The worst case was an old Kurd who had been hit in seven places. One bullet had gone in one side of his head and come out the other. He told everyone about it in lurid phrases, which carried conviction more from their forcefulness of diction than by any comprehension of their meaning. Before long, he and the others arrived back the village, slung across the backs of mules, to the care of Dr Christopher Columbus.

A rough goat-track led from the column's left to the valley of Ogaz, the hotbed of the insurgents. From here, an enemy with a Pathan's enterprise and dash would have come in on the Wurdi Major's rear, so I sent out from Bajgiran a small picquet to watch this for him.

Also, as Amal Baz was well aware, only a dozen miles away there lay an enemy force of 4,000 under Turkish officers. This constituted a grave menace; had it intervened, he would have had to fight his way out as best he might.

As they marched on, the valley walls closed in, and the column and its mules became exposed to the fire of possible snipers on the flanking hills. According to Field Service Regulations, Amal Baz should have placed infantry picquets on the hills to either hand, to cover the advance of his main body up the rough valley floor, but this was clearly impossible from the very few men he had in his force. He accepted his risks and devised a new method of minor tactics to deal with the new situation. He used his Lewis gun from alternate positions on each side of the valley to fire obliquely across it, and to cover the advance of his bayonet-men to drive the Kurds successively out of their sangars.

Soon enough the insurgents again made a stand higher up by some old ruins; the Lewis gun came into action obliquely from the south side of the valley, enfilading them in a manner most disturbing to their peace of mind.

The process was repeated until night fell, and the sweat-drenched, panting men snatched a few hours sleep where they lay, behind boulders or in crannies of the rocks, covered by a few sentries, whilst an occasional Kurdish bullet splashed on to a boulder and ricocheted humming into the night.

Before the first spears of dawn had glinted up from the Caspian, fighting commenced anew. Everywhere the Kurd attempted to make a stand, he was turned out by a nicely judged combination of fire, bomb, and bayonet. By midday Amal Baz had made good the crest of the pass, and sent me a very reassuring message to say he had done so. The last twenty-four hours had been an anxious time, for we had no real means of knowing the fighting value of the Kurd, or to what heights he could be brought. It was a grave responsibility to send out a column to tackle an enemy some seven times its own strength.

The column spent all that evening and well into the night hunting their enemy down westwards turning out small knots from rock clefts with the bayonet, taking snap-shots at retreating figures in the birch thickets, or sweeping defences with the Lewis gun.

Very early next morning the force arrived within half a mile of Namanlu, Khudu's headquarters. In the exchange of fire, the fine chestnut Waler horse that I had lent Amal Baz was shot. But from a range of fully 800 yards, the youthful lance naik who commanded the Lewis gun, took aim at the defenders. The Pathan is in the habit of dropping his man at ranges where European street-bred eyesight can see nothing at all. He judged it to a hair. A good burst from his weapon killed seven Kurds, who were the leaders and backbone of the resistance.

This so disheartened them that they refused to face the rush of our bayoneteers and bombers that cleared the village. The thatched roofs caught fire, the flames of the burning homesteads lighting up the narrow valley, and soon the mounted men were galloping over Kurdish fugitives into the outworks of Jiristan to join hands with their besieged friends.

By the time the sun was well up nothing remained in that green little valley to tell of the fighting but a row of stiffening Kurdish corpses laid out in front of the customs post, and black curls of smoke tinged with orange flame rising straight up in the still morning air from the homesteads of Namanlu.

Khudu's followers abandoned him in the next day or two: a small column of ours made a reconnaissance from Kuchan into the Ogaz Valley with hardly a shot fired at it. I went out next day with a platoon of the Pathans, whose role was to clear the valley of any wanderers. During a long summer day we swept the defiles nearly up to the pass, our little Lewis gun always handy. It was dark as we clambered down the rough trail through an outlying farmstead. Suddenly I came upon a tall, long-cloaked Kurdish figure, who eyed me for a moment in the gloom and remarked, 'Here's the head brigand himself!' This was a blow after our efforts on the side of law and order, but perhaps we were not quite as sleek and tidy as we would have been for a reception at St James's.

The various Khans who had backed Khudu came sheepishly to see us over a cup of tea, ingenuously explaining how they had been led astray by that horrible little man. What they really wanted was protection from the Persian authorities, who were far too solicitous of their own hides to tackle Kurds under arms, but were quite willing and ready to torture any whom our jawans might round up.

The General Staff of the First Red Army were disgusted with Khudu. They vented their spleen by sending rude messages to him at his castle near Gilyan requesting the return of funds advanced and of arms lent to him.

Khudu was soon encircled in his château by a motley assemblage of excessively armed and bandoliered Kurds who grazed their wild, long-tailed ponies in the lucerne and standing corn of the unhappy Persian peasants. But he slipped away during the night, doubtless with the aid of palm-oil. This was the last the world heard of Khudu.

A satisfactory feature of these little wars was the fact that my men had, at the cost of very severe labour, been able to map the ground over which the troops fought, and we were able to print off ferro-prussiate copies for all the platoon and troop leaders concerned. It is not always on the ground one maps beforehand that the enemy chooses to fight.

Soon I was back at my headquarters in Bajgiran, looking down on to the road which led up to the Headquarters of the First Red Army Division. When things had quietened down and all the smoke cleared away, there came up the hill a small party from the other side. They approached with courteous salutations and polite speeches, from which it appeared that the object was to offer me the rank of major general in command of a cavalry brigade in the Red Army, to wit, the First Independent Turkoman Cavalry Brigade. They were even so kind as to bring the badges of rank with them. I told them that I felt very flattered by their offer but hardly saw my way to accept. The badges of rank I kept, and still have.

After the operations were over, I received the following signal message:

> To Cdg. Bjn. Follg. recd. Begins aaa inform Major Blacker and Capt. Duncan that these private wars must now cease. League of Nations. Ends. For necy. action adsd. Cdg. Bjn. From force staff. – M.D.

Our official evacuation orders arrived soon afterwards. Very secretly, by night, we brought in our patrols and sentry groups, blew up a bridge or two on the main road and a revetment wall, and marched in the chill early morn towards Kuchan.

Some more riff-raff Persian infantry took over, and we felt very sorry for the convivial Hassan Khan and our Persian and Kurdish friends, in view of the Soviet's invasion that was now a foregone conclusion, as were the massacres that would accompany it.

Hardly had we marched out but the Reds seized a poor old strolling singer, a white-haired Kurd, who used to enliven our long evenings with sitar and song. They accused him of being a British spy. Then, putting a stake into the ground where a lonely goat-track crosses the crest of the frontier range, they nailed him to it, driving iron railway spikes through his ears. A couple of friendly Kurds found his body by chance a few days later.

We marched off with 600 camels, which grew to 1,600 as we collected stores from the supply depots along the way. The protection of this huge mass from possible Afghan raiders was hard work for the handful of troops. Every day my men were either advance-guard or rear-guard, whilst the infantry furnished flank guards and escorts for the horde of camels that stretched its weary length for several miles.

Eight hundred miles, at two miles an hour to conform to the camels measured tread, dragged out their interminable length. Every few days we would march into a town or village at midnight, and a day's halt relieved the brain-numbing that long night marching causes. One's mind gradually gets inured to the monotony, and in a month or so a ten-hour march seemed shorter than a four-hour journey had been before. Such is the effect of the imagination.

We got to the railhead, and at last the dusty train, which seemed to have square wheels, drew into the Quetta station and our long trail was ended.

Indian Army Headquarters eventually decided to give us all a medal for the Bajgiran campaign. This was very acceptable, because Indian Army Instruction No. 84 of 1926 designated it under my own name. I believe I must have been the only captain to have an independent command in the First World War. It took a very long time to come through, in fact those six years, because the decision had to be referred to the War Office, who had difficulty in believing that there was in fact a Kurdistan in those remote parts beyond the Caspian Sea.

Our last long march from the Russian frontier was but a very small portion of our three years' odyssey in Turkestan and Khorasan. My little detachment could not have covered much less than 9,000 miles in these years, excluding railway journeyings. This march over innumerable snow- and ice-bound passes, great glaciers, and illimitable expanses of waterless desert seemed formidable enough to us as we looked back to it, but we reflected how infinitesimal a portion it made of the eighty years' toils and journeyings of men of the Guides all over the heart of Asia.

Chapter 20

FROM WAR TO PEACE

Hostilities finally ceased, and in 1922 the General Staff paid me the compliment of a nomination to the Staff College at Quetta, which was then commanded by the great Louis Vaughan, whose views were considerably ahead of other generals of his standing in India. The other students were all senior majors, who had commanded not only battalions but, in many cases, brigades in the major theatres of war, mostly in France. The instructors were only slightly senior to them in service or experience, so the students indulged in a great deal of backchat and refusal to accept everything that the professors told them without demanding chapter and verse. It was all a very great testimonial to the freedom of thought which was allowed, and even encouraged, in the Army, especially under commanders like Louis Vaughan.

A fellow student, later to rise to high honours, was the famous 'Pug' Ismay, also a Piffer. Few soldiers played a larger part in winning the Second World War, or rather in preventing other persons from losing it.

After the Staff College the great honour was done me of an appointment on the Imperial General Staff at the War Office in Whitehall, a boon accorded only to a single Indian Army officer at a time. I found myself in the Russian Army Section of Military Intelligence. Besides Russia, we dealt with Poland, Lithuania, Latvia, Estonia, Finland, Sweden, Norway and Denmark, and so with all the cheerful military attachés of those lands.

An early excursion in May 1927 took me on an urgent call to Old Jewry, in the City of London, where I was to report to the Chief of Police. 'Come along,' said he, and a police car sped us to

Number 49 Moorgate, where there was already a cloud of pulverized concrete and that sickly, sinister smell of detonated gelignite.

This was the so-called 'Arcos Raid' on the headquarters in England of our Muscovite enemy, masquerading as a trade mission. 'Secret papers' had been 'accidentally' left lying around in the War Office to tempt Russian infiltrators. Sure enough, they went missing.

An Inspector waved us up to the first-floor landing, where sounds of conflict percolated through a part-closed door. Constabulary muscles soon pushed this open to display to us a plain-clothes City policeman and a Bolshevik locked in a tooth-and-toenails struggle on the floor. The detective was trying to prevent his victim from swallowing some documents.

This was successfully accomplished and we moved to a large hall, filled like a schoolroom with dozens of prep-school type desks. On each of these were Communist catechisms, instructional primers, correspondence courses in Marxism and so forth, from which the police gathered in the names of very many British converts, or would-be converts. From here we came into a grim, octagonal chamber, flush-panelled, with no windows whatever, so that once inside one could look round and see no visible way out. This was the Commissar's room, where he interrogated his victims, terrifying them by the feeling that they could have no escape. The picture of Lenin which had hung behind his desk had been taken down by a policeman, who had left thumb marks on it. This was an item of complaint in the formal protest made by the Russian Foreign Office, who reckoned it sacrilege.

A pleasing feature of my job was official visits to foreign armies in the lands of Northern Europe. Quite unforgettable on some of these was the hospitality of the Poles. This included opportunities to shoot, in the snow-clad forests, their great wild boar, who, unless deterred, savaged the peasants' crops. A single boar could destroy an entire potato field overnight, and he could weigh perhaps 500 pounds. So when my chance came to deter a promising specimen I was glad to have a .404 Holland and Holland in my grip.

There were military diversions too, of course. At Baranovice they mounted a very thrilling assault-at-arms, in which was a horse artillery competition. The teams galloped up on one side of a low thatched cottage, down the other, and then fired off a round of blank, in forty seconds. One could see, too, an Uhlan regiment of one machine-gun and five sabre squadrons cross a broad sunken road at a swinging pace, down a six-foot vertical bank and up sandy slopes beyond, without a single horse coming down.

My first visit took me to Gdynia, then hardly more than a fishing village, which had some naval hutments run by a grizzled boatswain and a dazzlingly beautiful young typist. At my next visit it had grown so much that an Atlantic liner could, and did, come alongside.

The Poles were our allies, or we should have been theirs, so we looked about to see how to help them. The answer was an amphibious landing of three British divisions between Danzig and Hell, an operation reminiscent of Hornblower, had that story then been written. In those days we could stand up, especially in Naval forces, to Russia and Germany, and be a help to our friends, whom we had to throw to the wolves in 1939.

Some ten weeks before our General Strike, duty took me to Vilna and to be a guest of its Provost Marshal. He had not long before, in the war with the Lithuanians, put demolition charges under all the important bridges; but, alas, could not remember where.

From Vilna, northwards in the snowstorm, the programme took me to Dvinsk, where the train halted under the grim parapets of their rugged fortress. There came to me alone in my end of the train a Lettish General Staff officer, who shook me warmly by the hand and congratulated me fervently in a rich Chicago accent.

'You British, they say you're slow, but, by gum, you can do things when you want to, in your quaint way!'

I accepted these tributes modestly, and by the time we reached Riga discovered what it was all about. It seemed that the express just before us, coming from Smolensk, carried a Russian delegation to London. As it slowed down, there sprang out of the blizzard a party armed with tommy-guns. The ensuing conflict in the corridors of the wagon-lit was bloody. The Lett frontier guard intervened to remove the corpses, and to take over three diplomatic pouches addressed for London. Of these, one contained bearer bonds insured with long-suffering Lloyds for a million and a half; the second had a bag of diamonds, apparently for the salaries of English Communists; whilst in the third were bundles of leaflets. These were to be stuck up in British barrack rooms, and told the British Tommy that he was being ill-treated, and commiserated with him on his horrid trousers and puttees.

At Riga, the General Staff felt that my denials of complicity in that bloodbath-in-the-snow were due to British modesty, and feared that Consul General Petrov would be out to get me. Therefore they gave me an escort of two Lettish full colonels of Herculean stature, each packing a pair of .45 Colt automatics in his trouser pockets. They showed me the night life of Riga, and as the early hours came along the full colonels got fuller and fuller.

But I got safely to Reval, alias Talinn, to meet traces of the coup d'état which the Russians had organized not long before. This began as a surprise attack by Communists against the dormitories of the Cadet College. The boys were slaughtered in their beds. Another party then came to the tank barracks with a forged letter calling for the ex-British tanks to be handed over. As the leading tank was being driven through the archway of the barrack yard, the Sergeant of the Guard became suddenly suspicious, and shot the driver. The tank slewed across and jammed the exit, so that no other tanks could get out, and the coup d'état failed at this moment. Estonia remained free, until the savage Russian seizure in 1939.

This tour took me on to Sweden via Finland. A novel and interesting experience was the short voyage in an ice-breaker to Stockholm, with a stop at Aland Island, where the postman drove up to the starboard gangway with a horse and sleigh.

In beautiful Stockholm one came into the pleasant monarchical atmosphere of Sweden. My kind host asked if I would like to ride a horse over the sea-ice. So next morning a chestnut mare came to the door and off we went over the somewhat alarming tramlines and frozen cobbles. But soon we were on the ice, and all was changed. The little mare was as sure of herself as if she had been on Rotten Row, and we galloped about as if nothing mattered. The ice must have been about six or seven inches thick, and one could feel its resilience under the weight of our two horses.

Next came visits to amazingly modernistic Swedish barracks and a demonstration, most astonishing to one used to machine guns, of cadets firing their Browning automatic rifles. The astonishment derived from the fact that they fired thousands of rounds without the hint of a stoppage. A dazzling flash of the obvious showed that this was due to the superlative quality of their ammunition. It was of course rimless, which struck a blow at the British mind when one heard that our Army and Air Force could not have modern rimless ammunition because our Chief Inspector of Armaments could not manage its measuring and gauging. Therefore we had to modify the Browning for the Royal Air Force at great expense, and the Bren too, so as to make both less reliable by virtue of rimmed instead of rimless cartridges.

From Sweden, a very pleasant outing took one to Norway and a field day on skis with the Battalion of the Royal Guard, whose skill on the hillsides was something to hold one spellbound. Very kindly they assigned to me a gigantic bugler, an Olympic boxer, who, with superb tact and consummate courtesy, hauled me without a smile out of every snowdrift into which I collapsed. As the snow swirled outside, we retired with a bottle of *Akevit* into snug little wigwams made out of canvas sheets which they carried on their backs like rucksacks.

Then back to London and the General Strike. The Zinoviev Letter alarmed the general public, but was no surprise to us at the War Office. Our friends in Europe had been giving us innumerable similar reports. Our old friend the Swedish Attaché asked us what all the fuss was about. 'We get these almost every week in Stockholm,' he said.

In 1929 my wife became the Mayoress of Westminster, so I was asked to civic luncheons, usually very excellent. At one of these I found myself sitting next to a young woman who seemed to expect some small talk. So I remarked to her that I much deplored the absence of thought in modern life.

She said: 'Just what do you mean?'

I replied: 'In the Army, where I now am, I observe very much writing, little reading, and no thinking. In the political world, into which I come in contact, similarly, much talking, little reading, and no thinking.'

She answered: 'Would you not say that the Prime Minister [Stanley Baldwin] did some thinking?'

Automatically I replied: 'What with?'

After a pause she said: 'I'm his daughter, but don't let that worry you, because that is just what we say in the family.'

Perhaps it was just as well that, after four years in the War Office, a whole year's leave had come my way. What better place to spend it than in beautiful and hospitable Poland? So my wife and I sailed down the Danube to Vienna, a truly imperial city, though Austria was now a republic.

We changed to a train on the way in order to look at the monastery of Melk, which seemed about as large as an ordinary town. This train did not arrive until darkness had fallen, and it contrived to leave our carriage short of the platform. When I struggled to get our suitcases out, the abominable conductor moved the train forward and frustrated all my efforts. My German was not fully adequate to tell him what I thought of him, but I did my best. So when we stopped at the next station, he called a pair of gendarmes, who drew their swords and told me to 'come along with us'.

Not far off was the grim-looking granite Bridewell. We marched in and confronted the sergeant major of the gendarmes. 'Tact,' I said to myself, and asked him: 'Am I under arrest?'

'Yes,' he said quite promptly, 'for hurting the railwaymen's feelings.'

Hastily gathering my wits, I said to him: 'You are, of course, a sergeant major. Here is my passport, from which you will see that I am a colonel.'

He agreed, blinking slightly. 'So,' said I, 'I need not tell you, as a sergeant major, that I am entitled to two colonels as my escort.'

He blinked again, but continued glassy-eyed, as sergeant majors do.

'But,' I continued, being very accommodating, 'I will do with only one colonel, and say nothing about the other one.' He wondered what was coming next. 'Therefore,' said I, 'if you get on the telephone to your own colonel and ask him to come along and be escort to me, I am sure he will do so.'

Sergeant majors function much by numbers, so very soon the Colonel of Gendarmes came along to tackle this odd situation. He turned out to be a most delightful person and no sort of 'ex-enemy', so when he began to laugh at our sad story, the sergeant major soon faded away with his sabre-bearing cops.

We all laughed, but then I pointed out that, even though the situation seemed comic, here we were, well into the night, with no dinner and no roof over our heads; whereupon he rang up the Burgomeister, another very charming gentleman. When we asked where we were, anyhow, the reply was Durrenstein.

'Do you,' I asked, 'always clap travelling Englishmen into dungeons here?'

So with reminiscences of Richard the Lionheart, a previous inmate of Durrenstein Castle, more laughter followed from one and all. The Burgomeister asked us to an excellent dinner and reserved the best suite in the best hotel for us. Something like a Guard of Honour of the Gendarmerie saw us off next morning, and we parted with expressions of the utmost bonhomie, and the determination, if we had to go behind bars, to do it in Austria.

Chapter 21

PREPARATIONS FOR EVEREST

Retirement in 1932 naturally stimulated ideas about further interesting and congenial employment; almost at once the name of Everest loomed up high and large.

The tradition connecting our family with Mount Everest is an old one, going back to the second Valentine Blacker, who in December 1822 was selected to take over the Survey of India. This Great Trigonometical Survey was the immense achievement which culminated in the discovery of Mount Everest, named after Valentine's disciple and successor.

Some 110 years after Valentine laid his trigonometrical foundation stone, an American major turned up with an application to the India Office to be allowed to fly over Everest. With much difficulty they persuaded him that Nepal was not a British colony held down by scarlet-coated Mounties, as many of his fellow countrymen thought, but an independent kingdom.

The Kathmandu Government had the application passed on to them and required certain guarantees and safeguards. They were naturally most apprehensive about the possibility of a forced landing on their territory and the consequent relief expedition which might follow. So they stipulated that the British Air Staff should shoulder the responsibility for the good and reliable behaviour of the American aeroplane. But in those years the reputation of American aero-engines was quite moderate, so the Air Staff politely declined.

Just then, however, Roy Fedden's magnificent Bristol Pegasus was showing the world what it could do on its nine supercharged cylinders. Here was an opening for British aircraft to fly over the mountain. From being just an idea the flight over Mount Everest became a project.

This naturally called for a plan, and who better to join in the making of it than Colonel P.T. Etherton? The task needed considerable mental equipment and the doggedness to bulldoze one's way through that dull and stubborn opposition with which England greets anything new. Apart from anything else, there was not a little objection to the scheme on the grounds, it seems, of *lèse-majesté*, or even blasphemy. Lots of good people thought that to look down uninvited on the virgin summit of the highest mountain in the world was somehow the act of a 'Peeping Tom'. Etherton was the hero of tremendous breakthroughs in the Himalayas and China, and was a brother survivor of the storm and the taking of Neuve Chapelle in 1915. We had travelled together to Kashgar in 1918, and I knew he was the perfect man for the job.

Our first patrons and counsellors were the Earl Peel (my father-in-law), Colonel John Buchan and the Master of Sempill; with them and others we formed the corporate entity known as *The 1932 British Flight to Mount Everest*.

We soon came up against the grim financial obstacle of the world depression, still raging at that time. But then Etherton remembered that Lady Houston had come to the rescue of Great Britain when it became vital to win the Schneider Trophy from very tough Italian competitors. She had written a cheque for £30,000 with which Supermarine were able to develop their S2. Not only did this win the Trophy for us but brought a much greater result a few years later. The ungrateful public has forgotten not only this but the fact that the S2 was the immediate sire and progenitor, Rolls engine and all, of the Spitfire. The percentage of Londoners who expressed any gratitude to her for this when Goering had finished pelting them must be very small indeed.

Anyhow, we stated our case to her and another cheque arrived, which saved us, just as the Spitfire would save England from Goering.

The guarantee from the Air Staff was still needed. The first formal act was to obtain the blessing and moral support of the Royal Geographical Society, which, through its then secretary,

Arthur Hinks CBE, was always helpful and cooperative. Accordingly I submitted a Memorandum 'relating to a projected flight over the summit of Mount Everest,' to the Society with a covering letter 'to solicit the support and cooperation of the Society in furthering this enterprise, as a cooperation to scientific research'. The Expedition Committee considered the scheme on Monday 25 April 1932, and passed it with the cautious statement, communicated to the India Office, that 'they are of the opinion that in the event of Major Blacker being accorded permission to fly over Mount Everest, results of scientific and geographical importance are likely to be obtained'. It was enough. The Air Staff gave their guarantee and the enterprise got under way.

The Memorandum from the Society listed the objects of the enterprise as follows:

1. To reconnoitre and to map by air photographic survey the almost unknown southern slopes of the massif of Mount Everest, thereby making an important contribution to Geography, and to its allied sciences.

2. To produce a cinematograph film of exceptional attraction and real worth, not only to science, but to the world and education in general and to combine this with the creation of a new height record for an aeroplane carrying two persons, thereby adding value to both achievements.

3. To carry out these feats with purely British personnel and thereby to give a stimulus to enterprise.

These aims were all successfully accomplished.

It was Arthur Hinks who urged me to make sure of photographing the almost unknown Western Cwm. I was a little surprised at the time, when all climbing expeditions had been forced to approach from the Tibetan side of the mountain, because of the Nepal Government's ban on Europeans. Later on, I realized how farsighted he had been. For when, on Coronation Day 1953, the news broke that a New Zealander and a Sherpa had become the first human beings to set foot on that inviolate peak, there was nothing but rejoicing. Our successful photographing of the inaccessible Western Cwm, and plotting of it on a map was a small contribution to the accomplishment of that feat.

The way being now open, we had to consider the means. It was my belief that Roy Fedden's new supercharged Pegasus was the only engine in the world which could meet our need, which was to carry a heavy load up to a pretty good height. It was not merely a case of flying over Mount Everest, for that could have been done even earlier with a single seater. But a single seater could not have brought back any real scientific results, and a main object of ours was to show that the aeroplane, as an instrument of science, can go over and map the highest mountains in the world. (All this is commonplace now, but it was a real issue in those prehistoric days.) So with my hat in my hand and my heart in my mouth I approached the Chief of the Air Staff, Sir John Salmond, and asked for his blessing on the Pegasus engine and its abilities. It was forthcoming.

When the engine problem was solved, we needed an aeroplane, or rather two aeroplanes, into which to put our engines. Here fortune came to our aid and guided our footsteps to Yeovil and to Westlands. We were, and continued to be, immensely grateful to them, because those two staunch biplanes, which were provided for us, filled us from first to last with every confidence in them, and gave us never a moment of worry.

The question of fuel capacity was another of the anxieties of the flight, because, naturally, to reach the summit of the mountain we had to take every gallon of fuel very carefully into account from the point of view of weight. There was no margin; and the high wind velocities meant that we had to consume a great deal more fuel than was anticipated. Fortunately, this was compensated for by the unlooked-for efficiency of flying machines at great heights where they encounter so much less 'drag' than in the thick air of sea level.

By fuel I do not mean petrol, because quite early in our organization we found that a special fuel was necessary. Engines of this type, having a high compression, need an anti-knock fuel. Ordinarily, a considerable percentage of benzol is used for this purpose, but in our case the proportion of benzol had to be cut down because it freezes at temperatures of -60 Centigrade, which we reached in the early tests. The experts of Shell Ltd. produced a special fuel containing tetraethyl lead, which functioned admirably. Here, so I believe, we anticipated engine history.

Below the engine was the oil-cooling radiator. It might be thought that in the region of Everest no cooling device would be necessary, but we soon discovered that where the air is very thin, so few molecules of air come along to carry away the heat that a cooler of almost normal size had to be used.

All this, and the preliminary planning organization, researches and tests, took a whole year of very hard work, from February 1932 to February 1933. But at last we got two aeroplanes shipped to Karachi, whilst the personnel went by air, some in their own Moths and some in the comfort of Imperial Airways.

Chapter 22

CAMERAS FOR EVEREST

The next problem was the fitting of the camera, the vital piece of all the equipment. Those who are interested in the technology of all this will find it described in this chapter.

The central item for the flight over Everest was the heavy camera, mounted in gimbals pointed vertically downwards, for taking the continuous strips of photographs which we required for mapping. This was a Williamson Eagle camera, and was electrically driven from the main dynamo.

One of the major problems which confronted us with photography in extreme cold was that the celluloid of the film freezes and when celluloid freezes it becomes very brittle and flies to pieces if an attempt is made to wind or unwind it on and off spools. For this reason the cameras which employed films had to be heated very thoroughly indeed. This was done in two ways.

The survey camera consisted of three main parts: the film magazine, the camera body and the lens cone. Inside each of these items was fitted an electrical resistance heated by passing a current through it. However, that by itself was not sufficient. It was also necessary to blanket the cameras with fabric jackets, into which was sewn a network of electric filaments, through which was passed more current. In these ways, the cameras were heated both from within and without, and it took a considerable amount of current to keep them pleasantly warm. As well as maintaining the celluloid in a flexible state, it was essential to prevent the lenses from frosting over. Without heating, the latter, as we found from experience, would in a few moments become covered with a quarter-inch of frost, a circumstance not conducive to good photography.

All these heating elements had been fitted to the cameras, and the wiring connected from them to the spare magazines, also heated. Then there were the leads for the automatic electric drive. The whole arrangement became very complicated. Our thanks went to Messrs. Siebe German & Co. for conducting the experiments, which were quite advanced for those days.

Alongside the heavy camera was the drift sight. The navigator-observer looks down through the negative lens of this sight at objects on the ground beneath him, and is thereby enabled to tell to what extent the aeroplane is flying obliquely on its course. Rotatable parallel wires are fitted in a frame over the lenses, and by turning these until conspicuous objects on the ground appear to pass parallel with the wires the observer is able to measure the angle of drift. This is important, because, except in still air or with the wind dead ahead or astern, the machine must fly obliquely to its course, nosing slightly into the wind. It is necessary to rotate the camera to the same angle in the opposite direction in order that each exposure taken shall be square with the course, not with the central line of the machine. Had the centre line of the aircraft been kept on the mountain, the path it followed would have been a curved one which would have been unsuitable for mapping.

Unless this direction were taken, it might be difficult to get the details of each photograph to overlap with the next, and we had a film with 144 exposures on it, each five inches by five inches; so it was of vital importance that there should not be the slightest gap in overlaps, a number of these strips being pieced together to form a 'mosaic'. Each exposure and each strip is taken automatically, and they must overlap by 33 per cent or more to form a continuous strip. This matter of the overlap was one which caused us the utmost anxiety from first to last, because there were several factors which made it extremely difficult to guarantee the continuity of the overlap, and because the slightest break in this continuity would ruin the strip. A bank of clouds suddenly appearing below the machine or a valley filled with mist would make this break and spoil it for mapping purposes.

Worse still was the danger that the aeroplane might be tilted either laterally or fore and aft to such an extent that the exposure taken at that moment would not join to the one before. It is obvious that the machines had to be flown with the greatest skill and steadiness.

Our cameras were fitted with Ross's wide angle Ypres lenses, with which the width and length of the picture was equal to the height of the aeroplane above the ground. This was an achievement of great credit to the lens makers.

Besides the vertical pictures, whose interest was mainly scientific, we needed also the obliques. These were taken on Ilford panchromatic glass plates, for which each aeroplane carried two hand-operated cameras. Although in this case there was no film to be heated, it was still necessary to warm the lenses of these instruments and also the fabric blind of the shutter which, being of rubberized material, would have frozen. For each of the hand-held machines twenty-four plates were carried in dark slides.

The remaining piece of 'still' equipment was our big infrared camera, used not during the main Everest flights, on account of its weight and bulk, but on subsidiary flights. It was far too big to handle in the air, and so had to be fixed to the undercarriage, pointing forward; the dark slides were inserted by the observer lying prone and putting his head and shoulders through the floor of the machine. The space in the undercarriage was originally provided by the makers to take aerial torpedos, for which the P.V. Westland was primarily designed. We had to do a lot of experimenting before we got it right, and, curiously enough, I found that horsehair pads were preferable to any form of rubber to absorb vibration. Another great difficulty was that oil from the bottom cylinder blew straight on to the lens. I provided a flap to go over the lens whilst taking off, but this stuck in the oil and would not go back before landing; so when we returned to the aerodrome I found to my dismay and horror that the lens was completely covered with oil. However, to my surprise, I found that this made not one jot or tittle of difference to the quality of the photographs. Perhaps this is one of the properties of infra-red photography.

Finally there was the moving picture equipment. Both planes carried one cine camera each, made by Newman and Sinclair, loaded with 200 feet of standard professional 35mm film, with 400 feet spare. Each of these, and the spare spool boxes, had to be thoroughly heated in much the same way as the heavy camera.

A baby Cine-Kodak in the leading plane completed the outfit.

An important item in the comprehensive collection of instruments with was the Williamson intervalometer. This automatically made each exposure in the vertical camera after a predetermined interval, so that it took place at the right instant to make the picture overlap with the previous one. The interval depended on the height of the machine above the ground: the greater the altitude the longer the interval. On the flight, of course, the ground level came very rapidly upward to meet us, and as it came up we had to estimate the height and set the intervalometer accordingly. This estimation was extremely difficult, because, the main part of the ground being unexplored and unsurveyed, mountains of anything up to 24,000 feet appeared in quite unexpected places.

Chapter 23

FLIGHT OVER EVEREST

The machines were assembled and erected expeditiously at the RAF Station at Karachi, in a temperature of 100 degrees in the shade. After a fortnight's work there, in the very enthusiastic and efficient hands of the RAF, we started on our three hops across India to Bengal, from the extreme west to the extreme east.

The first was to Jodhpur, 500 miles from Karachi in the centre of an immense desert. The city is dominated by a wonderful mediaeval castle surmounting the crag, and everything is almost as it was in the fifteenth century, but not quite, because the progressive Maharajah, who himself loved flying, had created an airport which would be a credit to any western European city.

The next day we flew to Delhi, where we were met by the then Viceroy and his wife. It was impressive to see Lutyens' New Delhi from above, as we flew into the Delhi Flying Club hard by the domes of Humayn.

Our third hop took us over the great dusty plains of India to Purnea, 200 miles north of Calcutta. The inhabitants there had never seen aeroplanes before, and the Rajah of Banaili sent his elephants to greet us. He also lent us three motor cars and a lorry from his private fleet, indeed all that we asked for. Northwards from there, the independent kingdom of Nepal stretches up to the crest of the Himalayas, where we met the frontier of Tibet, and this led to Everest.

One of the great difficulties of the expedition was the independence of Nepal. The country had not, I think, been traversed by a European for over a century, so we had to get permission from the King and the Prime Minister. It helped, this being India, when someone remembered that the Lord Krishna had constructed and flown an aerial chariot. Perhaps, it was suggested, our chief pilot, the Marquess of Clydesdale, might be his reincarnation. At all events permission was granted.

So the technical difficulties had been surmounted by British designers, political and theological difficulties overcome by Etherton, and the financial problems had been solved by Lady Houston.

So far so good: but we now came up against meteorological difficulties. A wind of great strength blows from west to east at an altitude of 25,000 to 30,000 feet, which meant greatly increased fuel consumption. Our average air speed was 135 miles an hour and our plans had been based on a wind of 30-40 miles an hour; but still during March the winds raged at 90 miles an hour. So we waited.

Every morning one of our scouting Moths reconnoitred the three great mountains from a few thousand feet to see how clear – or not – they were of clouds. Every evening we waited anxiously for the weather forecast from Calcutta. Then, on Friday, 31 March the winds began to lessen. Monday dawned, an auspicious day according to the astrologers; the Moth reported the mountain crystal clear; the meteorologists pronounced a wind velocity of 58 miles an hour. We had decided anyway to risk a higher velocity of wind than we had planned for. What we should now call D-day had arrived.

There were seemingly endless, time-consuming but essential preparations, particularly the fitting of the cameras, which could be done only at the last moment because of the all-pervading dust at the aerodrome. Once they had been completed, we climbed into our heavy suits. We collected the mail which was to fly over Everest with us before despatch to King George V, the Prince of Wales, and Lady Houston, and lowered ourselves into our machines. The engines were already ticking over. At 8 am we took off. In the Houston-Westland were the pilot Clydesdale, and myself as observer; in the Westland-Wallace the pilot was Flight Lieutenant D.F. McIntyre, and the observer Mr R.S. Bonnett, aerial photographer of the Gaumont-British Film Corporation. The course was 342 magnetic.

Our oxygen was carried in four cylinders, each of 750 litres at

120 lbs pressure, whence it passed along copper pipe to a regulating valve. In this operation it had to go through a tiny hole, and one of the risks of flying at those altitudes was that, if there happens to be any trifle of moisture in the oxygen, due to passing through a cloud or any other circumstance, this will freeze in the hole and block it with a tiny plug of ice. This would cause the breathing operations of the crew to be suspended, and a suspension of thirty-five seconds would be enough to cause unconsciousness. This was one of the main risks of the flight. To avoid it, the oxygen was passed through an electric heater, and the security of the oxygen system therefore depended on the efficiency of the electric current.

In accordance with the advice of physiological experts, we breathed oxygen from ground level up, in order to acclimatize not only the lungs and the muscles but also the brain. There was a flow meter graduated, perhaps unexpectedly, in thousands of feet of height. The procedure was that at, say, 5,000 feet enough oxygen was released for that altitude and the opening was successively widened at higher altitudes until we inspired neat oxygen at 30,000 feet, which was necessary in view of the hard physical work to be done in handling the cameras. We found that by this plan not only did the lungs and muscles work satisfactorily but, which was more gratifying to note, also our wits.

Apart from the mental effort required to carry out the numerous jobs of the ascent, there was also the danger that the individual breathing oxygen would get his mind fixed on some particular thing to the detriment of his other tasks. This is one of the phenomena encountered when breathing oxygen: the judgment and perception are dulled, and the individual is apt to make serious, even fatal, mistakes. The danger lies in this being very insidious, so that the airman may not realize what is happening until it is too late.

We were also advised that concentrated oxygen could be poisonous, possibly causing convulsions or epileptic fits. We did not suffer from either, which was just as well, because either would have been most inconvenient at 30,000 feet in an open biplane.

Nearly all the instruments and appliances used in this expedition were of a new or specially modified type for the job.

Practically nothing was standard.

Some description of the crews' outfit may be interesting. Their boots, to begin with, were electrically heated, as were their gloves; indeed the whole outfit had electric heating wires sewn into it almost all over.

The goggles worn also had to be electrically heated. They were made of two thin sheets of glass with filaments in between, and the current had to be turned on gradually by means of a circular rheostat in order not to crack the glass. This warming of the goggles was important. We heard on investigation that when Major Schroeder of the US Army Air Corps made an attempt on the altitude record some years before, his goggles had come off and his eyeballs had become frozen solid.

Each man also had a telephone – but although there were only two instruments in each aeroplane, we still sometimes got the wrong number! The microphone was in front of the mask, and the earphones in each case were sewn into the helmet. Because the air is so thin at 30,000 feet that there is not enough of it to carry the sound for any distance, the helmet had to be fitted with the utmost accuracy so that the opening of the earphone was exactly opposite the orifice of the ear. Before starting from England we were tested in a compression chamber at Farnborough, and it was extraordinary how such noises as the jingling of keys carried no distance at all in the rarefied air.

By the time the whole outfit was fixed up, and the observer had his five cameras, spare spools and other things, he was connected to his aeroplane and cameras by means of twenty-two different leads and conductors, making it difficult for him to move without strangling himself.

All this will give some idea of what had to be done as expeditiously as possible on that spring morning in Bengal before the two aeroplanes became airborne. Nor was this the end of it. Once in the cockpit there were forty-six separate routine operations to be carried out by the airman photographer before taking off and during the flight. Mental concentration, as I have mentioned, being affected by the oxygen, it was necessary to have these listed and stuck up in front of one. They included such vital tasks as checking all the electrical connections, the heating and position of the cameras, and uncapping the lenses – as omission to remove the caps would ruin the flight, while in this dusty climate they had to be left on until the last possible moment.

At last all was done, and the two planes soared up through the haze over the brown plains of Hindustan. Everything passed off without incident, except that initially the dynamo refused to supply power. I had to take off the cover of the cut-out of the electrical system, undo the screws with my thumb-nail (we had forgotten the screwdriver), and press the platinum contacts together by hand. All was well, the generator now continued to behave perfectly throughout the flight, and a supply of current kept us warm from first to last.

After about twenty minutes flying we climbed out of the dust haze into the bright translucency of the upper air. To the right we saw Kangchenjunga in all its gleaming whiteness open out against the blue, for a few moments blotting out every other sight. Fumbling with the catches in my thick gloves, I threw up the cockpit roof and put my head out into the icy slip-stream. There over the pulsating rocker arms of the Pegasus was the naked majesty of Everest itself still far off, a tiny triangle of almost incandescent whiteness, surmounting a purple haze below and meeting the intensely blue sky above. Nearby to it were the sharp lines of Makalu, with its extraordinary hollow and great ridge, the 'armchair of the gods'. Everest was ominously flaunting its great plume of ice, and we could see the great cliffs of its South Face. Beyond, the mountains of Tibet began to show. It would be difficult to recapture or repeat the thrill of that moment.

As the Westland approached the peak, the plume left the summit and whirled down to the south, as though Everest had dipped her ensign.

Soon, very slowly it seemed, we approached closer and closer to the big white mountains, and all my time became occupied with work on the cameras. I crouched down over the drift-sight, peering through the great concave lens, adjusting the wires across it, and rotating them carefully to give me the angle of drift of eighteen degrees. I had to look to the spirit levels, longitudinal and transverse, and to adjust the tilt of the camera in both senses, until the bubbles rested in the middle of their travel. This required a certain delicacy and judgment as the aeroplane swayed from side to side. I glanced at the big aluminium actuating-knob, and

158

saw that after twenty seconds or so it turned by itself as the pilot had switched on the current into its motor. The camera was warm, the current was running through it, and all seemed well.

Now, lying on the floor of the aeroplane, I could move myself back a little on my elbows, open the hatchway in the floor, and look vertically down on the amazing mountainscape seamed with great glaciers, and interspersed with streaks of scree and shale. Then, shutting the hatchway and laboriously taking great care to keep the oxygen pipe disentangled and myself clear of all the various electrical wires, I could stand up and look again through the top of the cockpit. I caught a glimpse over the pilot's shoulder of the brilliant red light on his dashboard, which flashed for a moment as the camera shutter operated itself.

At these high altitudes the light had an amazingly penetrating effect, probably because of ultra-violet rays. I had to wrap up every slide in two coverings of black paper and place them in black boxes with spring lids directly after use.

Up went our machine into a sky of indescribable blue, until we came to a level with the great culminating peak itself. I was hard at work with the cameras, exposing plates, uncapping dark slides, winding and setting the shutters to seize a series of splendid views, and lifting the heavy cine camera to run off fifty feet or so of film.

I crouched down again, struggling to open the hatchway, to take a photograph through the floor. All the metal parts of the machine were now chilled with the cold; the cold of almost inter-stellar space. The fastenings were stiff and the metal sides had nearly seized. I struggled with them, the effort making me pant for breath, and I squeezed my mask on to my face to get all the oxygen possible.

I had to pause and, suddenly, with the door half-open I became aware of a sensation of dropping through space. The floor of the machine was falling away below us. I grasped a fuselage strut and peered through my goggles at the altimeter needle. As I looked at it in astonishment, it crept, almost swung, visibly, down through a couple of thousand feet. The aeroplane swooped downwards over a mighty peak of jagged triangular buttresses. This was the South Peak. In an instant we had lost 2,000 feet in this great down-draught of the winds, and it seemed as though we should never clear the crags of the South Peak on the way to Everest now towering in front of us.

However, the alarm was short-lived, for our splendid engine took us up through the great overfall. Again we climbed; slowly, yet too quickly for one who wants to make use of every moment. Our aeroplane came to the curved chisel-like summit of Everest, crossing it, so it seemed to me, by just a hair's breadth over its menacing summit. The crest came up to meet me as I crouched peering through the floor, and I almost wondered whether the tail skid would strike the summit. We swooped over the summit and a savage period of toil began. The pilot swung the machine skilfully around, back into the huge wind force sweeping downwards over the crest; so great was its strength that, as the machine battled with it and struggled to climb upwards against the downfall, we seemed scarcely able to make headway in spite of our 120 mph air speed.

I crammed plate-holder after plate-holder into the camera, releasing the shutter as fast as I could, to line it on one wonderful scene after another. We were now for a few moments in the very plume itself and, as we swung round again, fragments of ice rattled violently into the cockpit.

We made another circuit and then another as I exposed dozens of plates and ran off my spools of film. We could not, however, wait too long over the mountain-top, for the oxygen pressure gauge was moving downwards, an ominous sign. We had no very exact idea of the length of time our return journey would take with that violent wind blowing, and fuel was needed for emergencies. We spent fifteen minutes over the summit, and turned back. Soon we could see the serried peaks, row upon row in fairy beauty, outlined by the aluminium-coloured fabric of our rudder.

The 160 miles home passed surprisingly quickly. With another struggle I managed to change the magazine of the survey camera and adjust it to the drift now coming from the opposite side of the aeroplane. The second film in the cine camera, however, had become frozen despite its warm jacket, and was so brittle that I could not reload. My oxygen mask, too, had become a solid mass of ice.

In the other plane, Bonnet of the Gaumont-British Film Corporation, had stepped on his oxygen pipe and broke it; but while suffering great distress and pain, and even falling unconscious, he managed to patch it up again and continue his work.

Steadily we came down, gradually losing height, and soon the semicircle of gleaming peaks faded from our sight as the straight line of purple dust haze rose to overwhelm it.

A disappointment was in store on landing, when it was learnt that, because of the intensity of the dust haze over the lower mountains, our vertical survey pictures were not sufficiently clear for their purpose. We had always thought a second flight would be necessary, so now it certainly was.

The second flight over Everest took place on 19 April. The wind speed on this occasion was over 80 mph, and we could not fly straight to the mountain, but first had to fly westward for 100 miles and then turn to get the wind behind us during the second leg of the course. This procedure was successful, and this time we flew over the main southern ridge of Mount Everest, the ridge which connects the summit with Lhotse, its southern peak. Incidentally, this led us to the discovery of the existence of the immense westerly wind which sweeps along at those great heights, apparently across the whole of Asia, for most of the year. But for the existence of this wind we could not have got to Everest at all on that day, because the flight involved covering something like 400 miles, which was the ultimate limit of our fuel capacity.

We hastened, in breathless anxiety, to develop our vertical photographs, and, to our great joy, they came out extremely well. Each one overlapped with the next, and the strips, contrary to the forebodings of the experts, were continuous.

When all was over, we remembered that our Westland aircraft had been designed as torpedo bombers. In the Cycle of Cathay this was the year of the 'iron water birds'.

Then, stimulated and exhilarated by the magic visions of those high levels and the transcendent whiteness of the great mountains, we bade farewell to the many Indians, from rajah to ryot, who had welcomed, cheered and entertained us most nobly. But when we came galloping to Calcutta, we were brought down rudely to a financial earthiness, to meet a legal call from London, where an avalanche, or maybe a whirlwind, of writs was ready to fall.

It appeared that someone in Lady Houston's entourage had persuaded her that our second flight was an infraction of her wishes, based on the idea that our pilots must not be exposed to unnecessary risk. I have no idea what could have been the motives behind this manoeuvre, but we discovered our funds in London frozen and bills to pay.

As good luck would have it I found Lady Houston's solicitor, one Willie Graham, to be a most fair-minded and reasonable man. I called upon him with the Field Service Regulations of the Army in my pocket. To begin with, like most civilians, he was obsessed with the belief that our wooden-headed Army is cast-iron in its methods. Much to his surprise, I showed him those paragraphs, inspired originally by the Duke of Wellington, which lay down that a formal precise order must not be departed from when the giver is present. On the other hand, in the absence of the giver, and change of circumstances so require it, the recipient is not only permitted to depart from the letter of the order but is enjoined to do so. In fact the Army holds him to blame should he not thus depart from the order he has received.

When Willie Graham had got over this shock to his civilian instincts, he grasped the point and told Lady Houston to forgive us, which forgiveness took the form of large boxes of cigars.

Chapter 24

THE WAR BEFORE THE LAST

After Everest, in 1934, I was appointed Commanding Officer of the 58th Field Regiment of the Sussex Artillery in the Territorial Army, a job which enabled me to live in Sussex and to develop my ideas on ballistics and modern offensive weapons, which finally bore fruit in the Spigot Mortar or bomb projector, officially known as the PIAT (Projector, Infantry, Anti-Tank).

Before telling that story, however, it seems relevant to dwell on the record of British weapon production.

In the history of warfare it is difficult if not impossible to find an instance in which British forces achieved victory except with a novel weapon in their hands, and equally difficult to find an instance in which novel weapons have been the products of State armament factories, which so often seem to have been busy preparing for the war before the last.

An outstanding feature of the armament of Marlborough's armies was the excellent flintlock musket manufactured in quantity by Messrs. R. Brookes & Son of Birmingham and fitted with the ring bayonet, an improvement which the French appear to have neglected, to the undoing of their infantry.

In the Seven Years War the steel ramrod replaced the wooden one in the British Infantry. By virtue of this, and other improvements due to Nock and Manton, their rate of fire was increased so much that by 1793 Sir John Moore was able to reduce the earlier three deep infantry formation to only two ranks. It was this that gave Wellington such an important tactical advantage in the Peninsula, where Soult and Massena could never understand why they were outflanked by fewer men.

163

The British however, were armed with smooth bores long after they should have been. The disaster at New Orleans may be ascribed directly to the fact that the British smooth bore flintlock was out-shot by the long rifles of the Kentucky State Troops. A similar catastrophe took place at Gandamuk in the Kabul defiles in 1839 when a Regular army, 40,000 strong, marched into Afghanistan. Of this force, only Dr Brydon survived. The remainder fell to the long ranging rifled barrels of the tribesmen.

Although the Baker rifle was issued to a few Corps in 1841, the Russian war found the bulk of the British infantry still armed with smooth bores.

Immediately after the Crimean War, during which officialdom constructed an amazing 36-inch mortar, which of course burst, a loudly-expressed public opinion demanded up-to-date weapons. The attention of Armstrong and Whitworth were driven to ordnance invention. The result was a series of accurate weapons, which were much ahead of their time. They all discharged elongated projectiles with good fuzes and much accuracy from breech-loading rifled barrels mounted on carriages, which even possessed a top traverse. The Prince Consort coerced and bullied the British Army and the Royal Navy into adopting these guns in all sizes from 3-pounders up to the 7-inch 200-pounder.

After his death, however, our technical authorities, for reasons which appeared devastatingly convincing to themselves, took the bit between their teeth and decided to scrap these very efficient and advanced examples of private enterprise in favour of the Official Product.

The latter, it is almost needless to add, were muzzle-loaders designed by Woolwich and made of wrought iron, more remarkable for their weight than for their accuracy. This was in 1872, so at the Battle of Maiwand in 1878 the British Regular Artillery possessed only muzzle-loaders. The Afghan Artillery was superior in numbers and all armed with the rifled breech-loaders made by private enterprise, namely the firm of Armstrong. The Afghan Army won that battle with some ease. The British artillery saved their guns, but the infantry remained to be massacred. The Berkshires fought it out with bullet and bayonet to the last man.

The situation was righted swiftly by Lord Roberts. A special intervention of Providence made him the Commander of the

Army of the Punjab. Wonderful little man that he was, Roberts did not neglect the technical side, nor omit to put right the defects that Whitehall officialdom imposed on the Army. To this end he commissioned a certain Colonel Le Mesurier to design and develop the weapon known as the Screw Gun. Le Mesurier did not consult technical officials in the matter but went ahead and constructed the guns, at which they expressed much concern, leaving on record a pathetic protest that, far from being consulted, they had not even been allowed to inspect the finished pieces. This weapon was no small asset to the Indian armies in their campaigns which were fought in Afghanistan and on the North-West and North-East frontiers, and eventually at Gallipoli.

In 1881, a British Army, equipped with the small arms of officialdom, was soundly defeated at Majuba, by a Boer force that had provided itself with the designs of Westley Richards which they had purchased while still British subjects.

British Official Technical Design was not, however, it is fair to add, outclassed either by the Zulus, or by the Hadendowas, commonly known as the Fuzzy Wuzzies.

The Boer republics resumed their technical lesson to HM Land Forces in 1889, when they demonstrated the superior performance of the clip loading privately made Mauser over the box-magazine of official Enfield, and of the quick-firing designs of Krupp over the antiquated 12- and 16-pounders of Woolwich.

When the Boers went to war with us in 1899, they provided themselves with weapons which were superior at all points to those of the British Army. Opposing the box-magazine Lee-Metford they had extremely accurate charger-loading Mausers, and instead of our very few early Maxim guns with brass water-jackets on quite unsuitable wheeled carriages, they provided themselves with one-pounder pompoms. The British field artillery was armed with an antiquated 15-pounder gun, which would have been fully up-to-date at Maiwand twenty years before. Even though it was a breech-loader, it was completely outclassed by the quick-firing guns of the South African Republics. To crown everything, these enterprising Dutchmen had heavy modern artillery to which the British Army could oppose nothing at all. Nothing, in fact, until Captain Percy Scott of the *Powerful* improvised a few wooden field carriages with traction engine wheels, on which he put his long-range 4.7s and, hitching them to immense teams of oxen, brought them up to help in the relief of Ladysmith. The only quick-firing guns on the British side were the handful landed by the Navy, and the few batteries purchased by private contributions for the units manned by the Volunteer Force and the Honourable Artillery Company.

It was the Volunteer Infantry too, a battalion of the London Regiment, who pioneered in the matter of machine guns, again by private subscription, against an official ban.

Maiwand was not the last disaster that the official muzzle-loading gun inflicted on the British soldier and sailor. The Emperor William II of Germany was stimulated to a long career of *Schadenfreude* when he appeared at the Spithead Naval Review in 1889 flying his flag at the head of a Squadron of Battleships, all armed with Krupp breech-loaders, and found the Royal Navy mounting muzzle loading guns everywhere.

This ambitious man said to himself, 'Well, if that's the best Grandmother and the British Navy can do, there is every reason why we should ourselves start to build a High Seas Fleet, and reduce Britannia from everlastingly and tediously ruling the waves.' The culmination of this line of thought happened at Jutland, still a bitter and controversial memory.

The Maxim gun found its way into warfare, after War Office rejection, when it was purchased by a joint stock Company, the chartered Company of South Africa, to use against business rivals in Matabeleland in 1893. At last in the South African War of 1899 the British infantry regiments had one Maxim gun each, although of pretty antique design it is true.

Just about this time, the witch-doctors of Woolwich adopted the wire gun, which had been advocated by Mr Longridge in 1860, and during the forty subsequent years. The wire gun was mounted on a large pair of wheels and had a shield in front of it. This made it a sitting duck for the up-to-date automatic 1-pounder pompoms used by the Boers.

In 1900, British howitzers of Woolwich design bombarded Cronje's trenches at Paardebery with shells filled with official lyddite. The fuzes were also official, therefore few of the shells detonated properly, but merely exploded in a feeble and incomplete fashion, giving off great volumes of a heavy inert gas, fatal to life. It was indirectly because of this that the Germans justified, at least to themselves, their use of cloud gas at St. Julien on 23 April 1915.

Stung into doing something after the ignominious defeats at Maiwand, Colenso, and the Tugela, the British Government made Lord Haldane Secretary of State for War. His Lordship at last went in for quick-firing guns, and under the aegis of that mighty intellect we, at least, had 18-pounder quick-firers in 1914. But that same massive brain did not go so far as to provide ammunition for them and the French sardonically called them *'L'artillerie de deux coups par piece.'* They were indeed the only field guns in Europe which had no high-explosive projectiles. Even the Russians, who were supposed to be backward in these matters, started with a good supply of high explosive for their quick-firing artillery, of which they had fifty-two guns in each division.

The British government managed almost equally thorough results with the machine gun, and ruthlessly scrapped a tank designed by Robert McFie (whom I had known at Brooklands in 1914).

An amazing 'official' hand grenade actually existed before August 1914, of portentous cost and equally portentous nomenclature. The bravest bomber steered clear of it and improvised his own, until Mills came upon the scene in late 1915.

The Stokes Mortar was turned down by Ordnance Officialdom as crushingly as had been the Maxim gun in its time. Mr Lloyd George, however, got it into the army by dissolving the official committees and constituting a Trench Warfare Board, who obeyed his behests.

The Royal Flying Corps suffered as much as the Land Forces, because it was landed with a monstrosity almost beyond the conception of present day airmen, to wit the BE2c, a machine which embodied the quintessential spirit of a government department. The aircraft was, in the interests of foolproofness, completely stable, and therefore was almost unmanoeuvrable. It was very strong so as to be unbreakable in the air, but this made it so slow that it became the 'Fokker Fodder' of 1915 and 1916, until the privately constructed Sopwith restored British ascendancy in the air over the Somme.

Private enterprise then took a deep breath, and like a giant refreshed, put the tank into the Battle of the Somme. The tank, had of course, been turned down with record breaking promptitude by the technical brass hats when first it swam into their ken, and on every other occasion. That its development, under the quasi-filibustering stimulus of Mr Churchill, when it definitely was not his business, and how the work was done by a handful of non-regular, in fact very irregular, Naval Air Service and RNVR Officers, is almost forgotten, but needs to be remembered.

The enterprise of the earlier firms was followed up by that of Messrs. Vickers in such good style that by 1923, before the momentum of the Great War had faded out, the Royal Tank Corps possessed a weapon, in the shape of the 'Medium C' tank, superior by a head and shoulders to that of any other country.

Providence, however, must have been temporarily diverted from, or quite worn out by its onerous job of protecting the British soldier from the bureaucrat. Despite extracting vast sums from the pockets of the payers of the King's taxes, our army, almost alone in Europe, possessed no sub machine guns, no percussion grenades, no rimless cartridges, and no 'ultra bullets' for its infantry. Its field artillery had received no armour piercing shot to stop a tank attack, whilst the design of its anti-tank gun constituted a sample of official crassness only equalled by that of the BE2c. The shields of both anti-tank and field guns were thick enough to stop Boer rifle bullets, but not the bullets fired by Hitler's heavy tank machine guns of 1939.

The light machine gun though of private design had been entrusted as to its production to a Government Factory. There were not, of course, enough to go round. The Royal Air Force had, of course, no cannon in 1939. Officialdom handled that. The British Tank Force had also been bureaucratized, and so hardly existed.

In fairness to the experts of Woolwich and Enfield it must be conceded that they had evolved by 1939 for the King's Army quite the best lances, swords and bayonets in the world. The lance, of 1865 pattern, with its shaft of male bamboo and its superbly tempered head is unique and has no rival. The cavalry sword of 1908 pattern, the only pure thrusting sword of any cavalry in the world is the creation of an artist in design, of craftsmen in the making, of the world's finest steel makers in material and of a proof and inspection beyond praise.

Need we add that in 1939, in the matter of boots, saddlery, horse shoes and probably of pick, shovel and tent mallets, the British Ordnance had little to fear by comparison with any in the world.

Providence and private enterprise saved the country in September 1940 from an invasion and conquest similar to that which the archers of the Duke of Normandy had inflicted on English pike men and Saxon axe men in 1066. The Hawker Hurricane, that thoroughbred descendant of the victorious Sopwith line, and the Supermarine Spitfire, the progeny of Lady Houston's Schneider Trophy winner, each with their eight speeded up Colt Brownings, alone stood between the Bohemian corporal, the stone of Scone and the crown of Charlemagne.

Chapter 25

ANTI-TANK DEVELOPMENT

At the beginning of the Second World War the two anti-tank weapons in use by the British Army were the Boyes Rifle and the 2-pounder artillery gun. The Boyes was a copy of the large 12-mm Mauser, which had been hastily evolved by the Germans to meet our tanks in the First World War; and it took about twenty years for this copy to reach the hands of the British soldier. When it did finally get there, it was of no use because it was not able to penetrate the armour of an enemy tank. It was not even useful for firing salutes at funerals, because it had no blank ammunition.

The 2-pounder on the other hand was quite reasonably powerful and for once was provided with plenty of ammunition. It could have penetrated the armour of most of the German tanks opposed to it, had not the official designers repeated the mistake they had made in 1899 and stuck it high up on wheels. Not only that, but they provided it with a shield so that the German gunners could hardly miss it. No wonder the 2-pounder got hit by the Germans more often than the other way round, and gave rise in 1940 to the emission of a great deal of crude barrack-room language.

The 25-pounder of 1915, with which the field artillery was armed, was in fact powerful enough to knock out the German Panzer-Kurz III tanks. In 1939 it was intended that the 25-pounder should have armour-piercing solid shot, but unfortunately the War Office or the Ministry of Supply, whichever it was, omitted to supply the shot. Hence enemy tanks were not knocked out which otherwise might have been, and France was lost. The battered remains of the British

Expeditionary Force came back from Dunkirk to England, and had the effect of shaking up Whitehall considerably, so that anybody who dealt with the Panzer-Stuka menace at last received a hearing.

In the second half of the 1930s I had taken out patents for a much simplified version of the PIAT, which was so simple that it could be understood even by our technical officers.

One has to explain here that, the Bombard, its successor the Petard, the PIAT and the Naval Hedgehog, were what are known as spigot weapons.

Now the popular, and in fact the official, idea of a gun is a metal tube out of which one shoots a projectile. Contrariwise, this spigot weapon was not a tube. Instead it was the projectile that was a tube, having a tubular tail which slipped on over the spigot.

Quite early in the First World War the Germans produced a spigot-type of mortar, the *Grenatenwerfer*, which threw an 8lb bomb with a tail quite effectively. In fact there is good evidence to show that it contributed to the disaster which befell the Fifth Army in March 1918. However, the *Grenatenwerfer* – grenade-thrower – was a clumsy and primitive form of spigot weapon, and suffered from an astonishing technical blunder, which it is difficult to imagine the Germans making. This resided in the fact that there was no gas seal between the projectile and the spigot. Hence it was inaccurate and clumsy.

My spigot weapons all possessed a completely efficient gas seal, which took the form of a soft brass cartridge case which expanded by the force of the explosion into the tail tube, thereby sealing any possible gas leakage. It took a long time for technical officialdom to understand this, although it made the inaccurate and clumsy *Grenatenwerfer* into a weapon of the greatest precision and accuracy.

The other circumstance which made the Blacker Bombard so effective, and so much liked by the fighting troops, was the development by Imperial Chemicals of their 808 blasting gelatine which was the pet of young Lord Melchett.

At the same time as these ideas were germinating I had the good fortune to join the board of Parnall Aircraft, which had become a public company whose purpose was to build and develop the hydraulic gun turret for aircraft invented by Archie Frazer-Nash.

171

Chairman of the Board was Sir Louis Vaughan, my old commandant at Quetta Staff College. Parnall Aircraft, a very small aircraft firm, had been mainly occupied in making rather odd aeroplanes for the Air Ministry, perhaps the most interesting being the Parnall Pete, which was designed to be launched from a submarine.

After Munich in 1938, production of hydraulic turrets expanded merrily at Parnall. During this time I devoted myself to the development of an infantry weapon which would enable the infantryman to defend himself against the tank; something which was very badly needed.

This weapon, under the name of 'Arbalest,' was very well received by the senior officers of the Army, including several Field Marshals and fighting Generals, but was violently opposed by the Ordnance Board, who stated that it stank in their nostrils. Even after it performed very well in firing trials at Shoeburyness in 1938 and 1939 it did not succeed in getting through the zareba put up by the technical bureaucracy. So it languished until after the Dunkirk disaster, when even the dullest official technician had to realize that something was necessary to stop the Panzer-Stuka menace, to which, of course, the official products – the 2-pounder and the Boyes rifle – were neither of them an efficient answer.

Chapter 26

THE BOMBARD

We were on holiday in Scotland when things began to blow up in August 1939, so I felt it incumbent upon me to hurry down south, and reached my Headquarters on that fateful Sunday afternoon. Here was my chief clerk hard at it. To my salutation he replied, being a Sussex man, 'Good afternoon, Zurr,' and to my enquiry about the state of affairs, 'Oh, it be a very uneventful day, Zurr.'

'But,' said I, 'There has been a war declared with Germany, I hear.'

'Oh, yes, Zurr, there be a war with they Germans, but it be a very uneventful day.'

My clerk was very busy entering up, in red ink, amendments recently promulgated by the Army Council to the Dress Regulations for Officers, a volume more sumptuous than any dealing with, for instance, firearms. The left-hand page was that dealing with the Royal Army Pay Corps. In future, should one of its officers be promoted to General's rank – a rare event – and should he take part in a ceremonial parade in that rank in full dress and – rarer still – mounted, then his horse was to a wear brow-band and rosettes of lemon yellow. On the right-hand page similar instructions were laid down for an officer in the Army Dental Corps except that his horse had to wear green.

In due course my territorial regiment went to the war, but I could not go with it, being fifty-two and over age. In due course it came back again. By that time, with Dunkirk in progress, I had finished my five years in command, and was relegated to hospital on account of the effects of wearing a steel helmet on top of a fractured cervical vertebra. I was convalescing at home when an urgent telephone message came from the Grand Barracks at Woolwich telling me to report there at once.

I said, 'All right, I'll come along tomorrow.'

'We want you to come along today,' said the Adjutant.

So I packed up my simple belongings and reported myself to the Adjutant's office. I enquired what I was wanted for, and was told that the matter was highly secret and I could not be told. Slightly flummoxed, I recalled my thirty-six years of service and experience of Army ways, which told me to betake myself to the cookhouse of the above-mentioned barracks, where I found matters being conducted by another very old soldier, Sergeant Cook. He, being an Irishman, was not hidebound by red tape, and so when I asked him what I was there for, he said:

'They want you take a ship over to Dunkirk.'

'What sort of ship?' I asked.

'A big ship,' said he. 'You've got an Adjutant, a Quartermaster and a Chaplain, and it will be on two hours notice. But don't tell anybody I told you.'

The 'two hours' went on and on, day followed day, the days dragged into weeks, punctuated by the arrival of some of my own officers with the tar of Dunkirk jetty still on the seats of their trousers. It soon became clear that there were no British troops left to bring back from France, and in any case the ships that were transporting them became smaller and smaller, far below the dignity of a lieutenant colonel. In fact they were being commanded by lance corporals or amateur yachtsmen. Meanwhile I was out of a job.

Nobody seemed to know quite what to do with a time-expired territorial colonel of advanced age, until I met my friend from India, General Ismay, who asked me what I was doing. I told him that the Artillery Record Office appeared to want me to go to Shanghai as OC Troops in a ship, an assignment which did not seem very attractive. So he said to me, 'Go up to the War Office and see Joe Holland, and tell him I told you to join,' which of course I did, and found General Holland an officer of really most advanced ideas, and astonishingly free from red tape.

Almost insensibly I gravitated into his organization, known, with the Army's passion for initials, as MIR, which meant Military Intelligence Research. This was divided into three

174

sections: MIR A, B and C. A and B handled the organization and administration of what were then called Special Service Companies and later became dubbed Commandos. MIR C improvised infernal machines, such as limpets or magnetic mines for attaching to the bottoms of enemy barges. This was being most efficiently run by Millis Jefferis, who had other devilish contrivances in his head.

It was dazzlingly clear by then that what the Army wanted was some means of stopping the all-devastating Panzer-Stuka combination which had swept everything before it. I pointed this out to several people concerned, including General Holland, and no one in the fighting services needed much persuasion in that direction, so I therefore resuscitated the idea of the bombard or spigot projector.

With the aid of the technical resources of MIR we succeeded in getting some spigot projectors made in a short time by that eminent firm of brass band instrument makers, Boosey and Hawkes, whose chief had lost a leg in the infantry in the First World War, and was therefore very ready to collaborate. He produced, with the aid of his firm, some prototypes which discharged portentous bombs, six inches in diameter and weighing twenty pounds, with very nice stabilizing tails, and filled with ICI 808 blasting gelatine which they were only too ready to supply in almost unlimited quantities.

We soon came to the point at which we needed some targets worthy of our steel, and found a British Matilda tank lying in a hollow on Chobham Ridges. It apparently belonged to the Experimental Establishment of the Royal Tank Corps. They had removed its engine and its gun, so that only the armoured hull remained. It was too tempting a target for us to overlook, so we drafted a letter to the Commander of this tank establishment asking whether he had any objection to our using his tank as a target.

We got no reply, so fired half a dozen shots at it and knocked it all into small bits, penetrating its 3-inch thick armour with holes through which you could put your head, and knocking the turret some ten yards away.

Unfortunately the letter had never been posted, and the next morning the Tank boys arrived to find their precious Matilda lying in bits, at which they were not at all pleased. All we could say was that, if it was so easy to smash up the Matilda, she was not much loss to anyone. This, however, did not appease them. Luckily they got into some trouble of their own on another front, which diverted their vengeful attention. Matilda remained in pieces, and the fragments are probably still there.

The next step was to invoke the interest of the Minister of Defence, no less a person than Mr Winston Churchill, who invited us to come along to Chequers to show him what we could do. A considerable audience of heavy brass, including General de Gaulle, was provided, and we banged off our bombard up a glade, landing its missile about 500 yards away and throwing up a very gratifying cloud of white chalk. Then they said to me, 'Now let's see what you can do in the way of accuracy – have a shot at that oak tree.'

This was disconcerting, because I had no idea really how accurate it was, and this was only a very rough preliminary prototype. In fear and trembling I pulled the string . . . and again this large missile cooperated by hitting the oak tree smack in the middle, causing it to tremble and give off showers of splinters.

'Excellent,' said Mr Churchill. 'Excellent, excellent. This is the artillery for home defence. Let's have 5,000 of them straight away. All right by you. General?'

Amid the congratulations of one and all, we packed up, feeling that our fairy godmother had come to the rescue and directed the missile really accurately where it did most good on the propaganda front. Then the real struggle started.

We constructed the Bombard by strictly clandestine methods, in the teeth of that embattled bureaucracy, the lineal descendants, through generations of unmarried mothers, of King Ethelred the Unready.

A signature on a dotted line procured for us a hidey-hole at 33 Portland Place. The occupant, manager for Radio Luxemburg, woke up one morning to find his building requisitioned. We soothed him by saying that his broadcasting was in abeyance anyhow; but almost the next morning Marshal Goering settled matters by dropping a large bomb on the place.

We had to grovel to officialdom in the form of getting the projector and its projectile blessed by the Ordnance Board, who detest anything novel. They were convinced that our 808 gelignite might perhaps blast a hole in mild steel but not in tough armour. The proof came in February 1941 on 'S' Range at Shoeburyness where, on a rise of ground, a crane deposited a great plate two yards square and three inches thick, of seventy-ton Naval steel.

'There, you old blackguard,' said the Vice President, a Major General, to me, 'Make a hole in that.'

We of the conspiratorial party smiled politely, put our heads down behind cover, and pulled the string. There came a vast bang, and a hole appeared in the plate, big enough to put one's head through, and situated to allow the winter sun to shine through its welcome rays. The Major General nobly ate his words and became an ally of our new armour attack.

High level approval was given, and we handed our great bundles of working drawings to the Ministry of Supply. Some days passed, and, convinced that the idea of perforating armour by means of 'cutting' explosives had taken hold in some minds, my thoughts reverted to the portable infantry form of the weapon, fired from the shoulder.

The Ordnance Board, however, was still convinced that a decent gun ought to have a hole down the middle. Hoping to combat this Gunner superstition, I went to see the Master General of Ordnance, who listened very courteously to my proposal to resuscitate what later became called the PIAT. When I had finished he said: 'It happens that here on my table I have the papers about these blasted Bombards of yours. It really looks as if financial sanction might be given to manufacturing them.'

As the recollection surged up of what Mr Churchill had said earlier, I gasped, 'Oh Sir,' seized my cap and stick, saluted, and staggered away, punch-drunk indeed.

Dumb instinct led me some 300 yards to Northumberland Avenue and the Headquarters of the new Home Guard, who had loudly demanded Bombards and plenty of them. I told their General my story, and he rang for his staff officers and their files. They explained that some weeks earlier they had minuted to the War Office that they desired to receive many thousand Bombards. The Permanent Under Secretary sent back a minute, which occupied several days in its passage over that 450 yards, enquiring whether ammunition would be needed for these 'equipments'. Home Guard HQ minuted back 'Yes,' and then, four days later, received another missive wanting to know whether the ammunition would be 'live'. Again the response of the HQ, suppressing sarcastic remarks about the invasion, was 'Yes'. More days passed, until the highly educated civil servant, very probably with a first-class honours degree, demanded to be told whether the projectiles would be filled with high explosive. Once more the Home Guard stifled its caustic rejoinders and said 'Yes'.

'In that case,' said the bureaucrat, 'storage accommodation will, we presume, be needed.'

Again the reply was 'Yes'.

'Then,' said the Permanent Under Secretary, chortling quite perceptibly, 'it is regretted that sanction cannot be accorded to the provision of these equipments, because we would remind you that Treasury approval was given to the raising of the Home Guard on the definite understanding that no charge would fall on the public for accommodation.'

Stung to fury and disregarding good order and military discipline, I cantered across to 10 Downing Street where I spoke to the Chief Military Secretary to the Cabinet, General Ismay. I told him all about it, adding that, if moving heaven and earth did not produce results, what about raising hell.

While the battle was on, and the officials still undefeated, I called on General McNaughton, the Canadian Commander-in-Chief, who had always supported progressiveness. He said, 'What do you want me to do?'

I replied, 'Order four of your second lieutenants to project the obstructer into that horse trough near St George's Hospital.'

He said, a little doubtfully, 'No, you can't do that.'

I urged, 'It is the clear duty of the daughter nation to help the Mother Country.'

Unfortunately, one of his own politicians had been hovering around, and created a sticky atmosphere. Often I wonder what might have happened. A court martial would have sentenced me to lose a year's seniority, but as I already had many more years than I needed that would not have been a big worry. The Canadian colonels would have told their second lieutenants not to do it again. But the shackles of authoritarianism would have been loosed quite definitely.

Meanwhile, however, heaven and earth had been moved, the climax coming when No. 10 brought about a grand demonstration at Bisley, whither the Small Arms School had moved. His Majesty soon decreed no less than 30,000 Bombards, with millions of projectiles for his loyal, and indeed welcoming, soldiery.

Note:

Blacker Bombards could be mounted either on a low steel frame or on a concrete emplacement, and were distributed to Home Guard battalions all around Britain. They were installed in strategic positions around the coast almost as far north as Scotland, ready for the expected invasion. Many Bombard emplacements, with the stainless-steel swivels on which they were mounted, are still in existence today.

Chapter 27

THE HEDGEHOG

Whilst we were grooming the Bombard to be ready for the troops, the Navy showed signs of comprehending the spigot form of attack.

In 1938 I had put forward, officially, a proposal for engaging submarines in this manner. However, in my 'Official obstruction' file is a letter from the Director of Torpedoes and Mining in the Admiralty, informing me that no naval staff requirement existed for an ahead-shooting weapon against submarines [conventional depth charges were dropped astern]. By 1940 a quasi-Naval organization had rediscovered the spigot system, persuaded themselves that they had invented it, and constructed at Chatham an ambitious form of it with multiple spigots. They were distressed to find, though, that when they fired it, their projectiles flew higgledy-piggledy and came down almost anywhere.

So a deputation came with it to our irregular red-brick villa establishment at Whitchurch, and met our most competent Quartermaster Sergeant Tyldesley. He at once pointed out the obvious failing, common to the German *Grenatenwerfer* of 1915, which was that there was no means of preventing the explosion gases of the powder from leaking in an uncontrolled manner between the spigot and the tube, which constituted the tail of the bomb. In the Bombard there was an all-essential brass cartridge case which expanded when the explosion gases forced it radially outwards, so sealing the gases completely and consistently. This was what made the Bombard so accurate in its shooting.

We soon found that the brass cartridge case of the naval 2-pounder pompom was just the size needed to fill the tail-tube of the Hedgehog, as it came to be called, due to its twenty-four bristling spigots. This expanding brass cartridge case made it an immediate success. Winston Churchill came to Whitchurch and saw it fired electrically, and its twenty-four great bombs distributed themselves with quite extraordinary evenness on the silhouette of a submarine marked out on the Berkshire turf. Once afloat, it gave immense satisfaction, even though, when mounted on the rather flimsy foredeck of those borrowed American 'four-piper' destroyers, it tended to buckle it slightly and to worry the Ward Room officers who had their habitat beneath it.

The Hedgehog, in a single eleven months period in the North Atlantic, sank forty-three German submarines, and in the Pacific an unrecorded number of Japanese. Because of its curious appearance, the US Navy called it a 'Rube Goldberg' weapon. This translates into English as 'Heath Robinson'.

Officers who used the Hedgehog told us that, in conjunction with Asdic and Radar, it was the dominant weapon in the Battle of the Atlantic. Here is how it was described by an American historian:

> The forward-throwing weapons . . . Hedgehog and mousetrap . . .sprayed a pattern of charges well ahead of the attacking ship, by spigot guns or rockets. These charges sank rapidly, and when one hit the hull of a submarine it blasted out a hole bound to be lethal. The weapon was designed to cover an area with a pattern of charges like a shotgun pattern, leaving no gaps, and thus shooting became more deadly. Most important it could be directed to one side or the other in accordance with the last-second sonar observations and could be fired while the submarine was still under sonar contact. (*Modern Arms and Free Men* Chapter VII, by Vannevar Bush, USA 1949).

And in more detail by Crowther and Whiddinton of the Department of Scientific and Industrial Research:

> The 'blind' time between the exact location of the U-boat and the explosion of the charges [during which the U-boat commander could sharply change direction and avoid the attack] is very much reduced by throwing the charges ahead. This technique was energetically developed in the early years

of the war. Mortars were introduced which threw ahead 24 projectiles each containing 31 pounds of TNT and fitted with contact fuses. The shape of the projectiles was designed, on the data of experiments with laboratory models, to be very quick-sinking, and the rate of sinking was thus raised to 22 feet per second. This weapon was called the Hedgehog. The mounting can be rocked by hand to allow for the roll of the ship. The charges are thrown in a circle of about 130 feet in diameter. Ships were fitted with this weapon from January 1942 onwards, and 48 U-boats were sunk with it. As the Hedgehog is fitted with a contact fuse it does not explode unless it hits the U-boat.

Because of the extreme haste with which it had to be put into mass production, there was no time for the experimentation needed to give it spring-dynamic spigots, which, as in the petard, would have made it much more powerful and with a lesser deck-load. Without consulting me, some official genius had the idea that a single one of the four rows of the Hedgehog's spigots would be a good armament for some of our landing craft. But what they overlooked was the recoil of this weapon, which, having not my spring-type spigot but fixed and rigid ones, knocked the bottoms out of these poor landing craft and got this Hedgehog a bad name.

In spite of the firm belief that no darned Limey can invent anything, the United States Navy was still using this in 1964.

Chapter 28

THE PETARD

The next of my spigot-weapons was vulgarly known by the troops as the Flying Dustbin. I called it the Petard, and officialdom called it the Mortar Recoiling Spigot, 29-mm. It was put in hand as a result of the sanguinary losses which the Canadians sustained at Dieppe in 1942. They had had nothing to make breaches in that formidable concrete sea-wall which was to prove so murderous.

So, after Dieppe, the Royal Canadian Engineers very sensibly experimented with the Blacker Bombard, which managed to smash up a good deal of concrete. However, when they bolted the spigot on to the turret of a tank it very contrarily bent with the shock of the discharge.

The experiments were being made on Wiggonholt Common, close to where we were living at the time. One evening a party arrived seeking advice on how to overcome this difficulty. The answer was a large spring spigot.

In fact the whole Petard projector weighed about four hundredweight, and constituted a good load for a tank, of which it became the primary armament, replacing the 2-pounder gun. It discharged a 40-pound projectile filled with plastic. Two of ICI's experts collaborated wholeheartedly, together with the Canadian Field Squadron.

We managed to mount the first three of these Petards in the turrets of three tanks within nine weeks, using not more than twenty pairs of hands. The Canadian Engineers organized a magnificent demonstration on Hankley Common against a great reinforced concrete wall, ten feet high, ten feet thick and a couple of hundred yards long. The first six rounds from the tank-borne Petard breached this formidable obstacle to such good effect that the tank was able to crawl through it. The problem was solved.

Another plan was also tested at the Hankley wall – the 'Double-Onion'. This involved 650 lbs of mytol attached to a huge steel frame like an overgrown garden gate. It was fixed onto the front of a tank, which pushed its grim load up against the wall. Then a bold Sapper, lighting a match on the seat of his trousers, lit the fuse and withdrew hastily. The fuse sizzled...then suddenly all the spectators, who were on a small knoll about 200 yards away, realized that they were far too close. When the 650 lbs went off and steel joists hurtled through the air, the extremely distinguished spectators, admirals, generals and politicians, went down amazingly flat in the mud. Large masses of flying steel just missed the director of the demonstration, whose microphone amplified his exclamations to one and all. Fortunately all the high Brass survived because the steel flew over their heads, but only just.

The Petard mortar, with its recoiling spigot, became the armament of the 79th Armoured Division, which was now commanded by Major General Sir Percy Hobart KBE. The wheel had gone full circle since he introduced me to plastic explosive in 1909, when he was the Subaltern of No. 3 Company of the Sappers and Miners.

Major Peter Selerie, in *The D-Day Landings* by Philip Warner, wrote thus:

> ... We then turned on to the road leading to Le Hamel. Pausing on the outskirts to check on enemy defences, we were overtaken by one of the AVRE Churchill tanks armed with a petard that looked like a short and very wicked piece of drainpipe sticking out of the turret. The sergeant in command said that he was the sole survivor of his troop and asked for instructions. I told him to follow our five tanks, remarking, in the words of the Iron Duke, as far as I remembered them, 'I don't know what effect you will have on the enemy, but by God you terrify me!'
>
> When we entered Le Hamel it appeared that the main enemy fire was coming from a large tall many-storeyed house. I ordered the Churchill tank forward to demolish the house

with the petard, which had a very short range. Maximum covering fire was given by the Sherman tanks' 77mms and machine-guns. The petard fired and something like a small flying dustbin hit the house just above the front door. It collapsed like a pack of cards, spilling the defenders with their machine-guns, anti-tank weapons and an avalanche of bricks into the courtyard.

The Petard, which as we have seen weighed about four hundred-weight and discharged a 40lb projectile filled with plastic gelignite, gave great satisfaction to the British and Canadian customers in Normandy. Unfortunately, the United States Army refused to utilize it, although it was offered to them for nothing. It would have been a great help to them at Omaha Beach where they suffered considerable and unnecessary losses.

Chapter 29

THE PIAT

In 1938 the most potent menace to forward Infantry was the armoured vehicle. Even the best of signals cannot make up for the loss of time involved in describing fast moving targets to someone even a small distance in the rear. The Infantry soldier needed to be able destroy a tank himself without delay, and not merely be avenged later by someone else. The Projector Infantry Anti-Tank (PIAT), light enough for a man to carry, quick to reload, and free from smoke, flash and blast, was the answer.

The PIAT fired a hollow charge projectile. The amazing principle of the hollow charge had been discovered by an American named Munroe in 1886. The high explosive charge was set into a parabolically-shaped recess which directed all of the force of the explosion forwards. This produced a jet of extremely hot gas and molten metal which could burn through several inches of Krupp armour.

It was Percy Hobart who, as a young Royal Engineer in India, had taught me about the hollow charge principle. Amongst other duties, he ran a class for infantry and cavalry officers about what was called 'Frontier Explosives'. Besides the regulation gun-cotton in its tin boxes, we had considerable supplies of commercial blasting gelignite, which leaked away from the miners at work on our huge Malakand canal tunnel. Percy Hobart showed us how a handful of blasting gelatine could blow the leaf of a plane tree into a steel plate by virtue of the hollow charge principle.

In 1937 or so, Woolwich and its research department had evolved a very feeble rifle grenade on this principle, known as No.

68. It could only perforate, with luck, one inch of armour, and this only at very short range. Later on, the task of improving the hollow charge missile was allotted to Churchill's Ministry of War Department MD1, which it did most efficiently.

Meanwhile, the work started by me in my own workshop at Whitchurch continued. Thanks to the super-efficient Tom Dale, watchmaker of Petworth, and the generous cooperation of Parnall Aircraft, we were building a demonstration model which could fire a hollow charge missile powerful enough to beat the Panzers.

Here Lord Cherwell took a hand, smelling, perhaps, some political kudos for himself. Moving through underground channels, he contrived that the unsuspecting War Office should sever the very tenuous bond which linked me to MD1. The official notification of this sinister move took a good many weeks to reach me, so some time elapsed before I discovered that Cherwell was running a rival. As one may see from the footnote to page 843 of *The Hinge of Fate*, he succeeded in mesmerizing Winston Churchill, who then gave the credit for the PIAT to Jefferis. Later editions, at my insistence, eliminated this mistake, the rival weapon having infringed my pre-war patents. Even Jefferis, who was particularly proud of this weapon, admitted that he had stolen the idea of it.

To return to the present time – in this case November and December 1941 – Britannia's fairy godmother had made Lord Beaverbrook her Minister of Production, and supplied him with an Australian Senator to his elbow, named very suitably, 'Trouble' Elliott. This Senator was too polite to say what he really thought of Pommies, but at once saw the qualities of my own projector when I showed him the village-made prototype.

Three more excellent projectors were made in double quick time, and shown at a meeting convened by the Director General of Artillery, Sir Edmund Clarke, who also had the Cherwell rival laid before him. Present too was Ewart Smith, Chief Engineer of ICI's Billingham Division. Sir Edmund Clarke, presumably remembering Solomon, said, 'Let the Service model embody the best points of either prototype.' And to Ewart Smith, 'Can you take it on?' The 'Yes' was enthusiastic, and soon the first fruits reached the Small Arms School at Bisley.

Then ICI took over and produced six prototypes of the spigot projector in the first six months of 1942. The first, Type A, was based on the Jefferis design, in which the spigot was separate from the flying weight, or sleeve bolt. After exhaustive testing, Type A was finally rejected on account of the fundamental weakness of the centre tube and other technical reasons. The second, Type B, was made from my design, in which the spigot and the sleeve bolt were rigidly connected together. Type C was a modification of Type B, with alterations designed to make the weapon more comfortable to use. Then they compromised between Types B and C to produce a lighter Type D. This was accepted in principle, and followed by Type E, which was the model designed for pilot production. Finally there was type MG, which, after some minor alterations to meet official requirements, became the official version and the ruling design for the projector throughout the contract.

Due to the Cherwell rivalry, we had lost eight valuable months. What with one thing and another, the projector was four years late into the firing line. If it had not been for these delays it could have been in time for Tobruk. In the end the PIAT reached the Eighth Army near Pont du Fahs at the end of 1942. This was almost the very spot where Scipio Africanus, by novel weapons, had defeated the Carthaginian armoured attack which before this had chased the Roman armies all down through Italy for ten long years. Altogether we had lost four years.

In this way the PIAT became the armament of the British, Canadian, Indian, Australian, New Zealand, Polish, Belgian, Free French, Netherlands, co-belligerent Italian and other infantries. The Russians got some too, but they did not, repeat not, drop them to the defenders of Warsaw.

Raleigh Trevelyan describes the PIAT in his diary of Anzio and Salerno in 1944:

My platoon has been given a PIAT, a curious home-made-looking weapon that I've never come across before. The bombs are like the headless bodies of outsize hornets, and you can send them between seventy and a hundred and twenty yards. The whole principle is based on a tremendously powerful spring. Every time you fire it, however, there is always that small suspicion that something will go wrong and that the bomb will fall short, just slithering out of the end of the muzzle. Yet the contraption fascinates me – it gives such a big bang and causes such a huge cloud of smoke; the Germans must think we have a new secret weapon. I take vicious delight in having my own back on those cold-blooded wretches who were lobbing rifle grenades at us – I can just reach them from here. The PIAT is a superb morale-destroyer; the blast must be devastating. Simon is amused by my enthusiasm and calls me Piat Trevelyan.

Then he vividly describes its use as an anti-personnel weapon:

At about midnight Corporal Peter whispered to me that he could hear digging to the right of Crocus. Together we edged up to our wire and, sure enough, the blurred shapes of a party of Krauts could be seen flitting about against the star-speckled sky. We hoiked the PIAT into position and aimed a bomb at the ground just below them. It was a beautiful shot. I'd never heard a PIAT explode with such a bang. At least half a dozen separate voices could be heard sobbing and moaning afterwards. Evidently the other Germans at Crocus were too afraid to fetch back their wounded, as we heard these wretches crying out for at least an hour.

The PIAT helped to earn several Victoria Crosses, one for Fusilier Jefferson, aged twenty-two, of the Lancashire Fusiliers, who was the only man in his Company who had never fired it before. He won it on 16 May 1944, during an attack on the Gustav Line. His battalion was left on its own, half dug in, to face a counter-attack of infantry and two Mark IV tanks. On his own initiative Jefferson picked up a PIAT, ran forward in the open under a hail of bullets, and destroyed the first tank. He then reloaded and went towards the second tank, but it withdrew before he could get within range. Soon after, help arrived and the enemy counter-attack was smashed.

Another VC came to a Gurkha, Rifleman Ganju Lama, in Burma on 12 June 1944. He was eighteen and a half years of age, four feet eleven inches in stature, and eight and a half stone in weight:

During a Japanese attack in May 1944 in Burma, Ganju Lama used his PIAT to blow up two tanks, for which he was awarded the Military Medal.

Four weeks later, the Japanese put down an intense artillery and airborne barrage, following by a tank and infantry attack. Lama's company were ordered to counter-attack. Initially good progress was made, but enemy tanks firing their main guns caused their attack to falter.

Rifleman Lama had the chance to lead an offensive against six Japanese tanks. It was dangerous because they were advancing in an open field with clear view and could crush anything. They spotted Lama and during the ensuing conflict fired on him, breaking his leg, his wrist, and wounding him in both hands. Nevertheless, he crawled on through slick mud, bleeding profusely, dragging his weapon and ammunition. When he came within thirty yards of the first tank he set up his PIAT, fired, and saw the tank go up in flames. He somehow managed to reload his weapon and fire again, accurately destroying a second tank. The tank crew survivors crawled out and came towards him 'bayonets glinting in the sunlight.' With one finger almost severed and hands slippery with blood, he threw grenades at the enemy, removing the pins with his teeth. Then, his ammunition exhausted, he crawled back for more projectiles. He attempted to destroy a third tank but it had taken cover. Another was shortly destroyed by an anti-tank gun supporting the counter-attack, and the remainder retreated.

Here is the story of Major Robert Cain, who also earned a VC while using the PIAT:

In mid-September 1944, airborne forces were attempting to capture the bridge at Arnhem. Major Robert Cain commanded a company of the South Staffordshire Regiment. His men landed eight miles from the 'Bridge Too Far' where the British were fighting desperately to retain their foothold.

Upon landing the South Staffords were soon being heavily attacked by tank and self-propelled guns, but they weren't able to bring up any anti-tank guns to repel them. Mortars were effectively being fired at point blank range upon German infantry, and the Staffords had to rely on PIAT's to deal with the armour. Lieutenant Georges Dupenois kept several tanks at bay with his PIAT, while Major Jock Buchanan and Cain drew a lot of enemy fire by running around searching for ammunition for him. Cain did not believe that any tanks were actually disabled during the action, but the hits did encourage them to withdraw. The PIAT ammunition ran dry at 11:30, and from then on the tanks had free reign over the area and proceeded to blow the defenceless troopers out of the buildings they occupied. The South Staffords were then ordered to withdraw from what Cain later described as their Waterloo.

Falling back through the 11th Battalion, Major Cain informed them that the tanks were on their way and requested they give him a PIAT, though sadly they had none to spare. He withdrew his men beyond the Battalion and gathered all the remaining South Staffords under his command.

Lieutenant-Colonel George Lea then ordered Major Cain to capture the nearby high ground to lend support to their own attack. This they did, but the ground was too hard for the men to dig in. They were soon spotted and came under very heavy mortar fire, and took many casualties.

The 11th Battalion were also cut to pieces by tanks and mortars. Only 150 men managed to get away from the slaughter. Lea was wounded and captured.

After he saw the destruction of the 11th Battalion, Cain took the decision to withdraw his men, now numbering only 100. 300 of his men had lost their lives. He later wrote in his diary: 'For the first time since childhood, tears sprang in my eyes. I turned away, swallowing hard and with rage in my heart.'

Cain now developed an intense loathing of tanks after these bitter experiences, and he personally saw to it that as many were destroyed as possible. If ever armour approached then he would grab the nearest PIAT and set out to deal with it himself.

On 20th September two Tiger tanks approached the area

191

held by South Staffords and Major Cain went out alone to deal with them armed with a PIAT. He lay in wait in a slit trench while Lieutenant Ian Meikle of the Light Regiment gave him bearings from a house above him. The first tank fired at the house and killed Meikle, while the chimney collapsed and almost fell on top of Major Cain. But he held his position until the tank was 20 yards away, whereupon he fired at it. The tank immediately halted and turned its machine gun on him, wounding him. He took refuge in a nearby shed from where he fired another round, which exploded beneath the tank and disabled it. The crew abandoned the vehicle and all were gunned down as they bailed out. Cain fired at the second tank, but the bomb was faulty and exploded directly in front of him. It blew him off his feet and left him blind with metal fragments in his blackened face. As his men dragged him off, Cain recalls yelling like a hooligan, calling for somebody to get hold of the PIAT and deal with the tank. One of the Light Regiment's 75mm guns was brought forward and it blew the tank apart.

Half an hour later though, Cain's sight returned, and against doctor's advice he refused to stay with the wounded and declared himself fit for duty. He also refused morphia. Instead he armed himself with another PIAT and went in search of tanks. Tigers continued to harass the force, and upon hearing that another was in the area, Major Cain raced out to an anti-tank gun and began to drag it into position. A gunner saw him and ran over to assist, and the two men succeeded in disabling it. Cain wanted to fire another shot to make sure that it was finished off, but the gunner informed him that the blast had destroyed the gun's recoil mechanism and it could no longer fire.

On Friday 22nd, his eardrums burst from his constant firing, but he continued to take on any tanks he encountered, contenting himself with merely stuffing pieces of field dressing into his ears.

Monday 25th saw very heavy fighting in the area occupied by the Force. Self-propelled guns, flame thrower tanks, and infantry took great interest in Cain's position. By this time there were no more PIAT's available to the Major, so he armed himself with a two inch mortar.

By the end of the Battle, the South Staffords had given no ground and driven off in complete disorder an enemy of 6,000 German troops armed with tanks, rocket launchers, and 100 heavy guns. Cain himself had been responsible for the destruction or disabling of six tanks, four of which were Tigers, as well as a number of self-propelled guns.

He was awarded the Victoria Cross; the only man to receive this medal at Arnhem and live to tell the tale.

In North Africa the first troops to use the weapon were the 4th Indian Division, who reported much in favour, having smashed up several Panzer-Kurz III's and discovered its value as a phenomenally accurate mortar. Sad to say, however, at the siege of Tobruk, rumour has it there were a couple of hundred in the Ordnance Depot there, whose commanding officer did not know what they were. So they were not used to beat off that famous armoured attack.

The Russian Army had sent a delegation of colonels to Bisley whom we entertained in the Army Rifle Association hut. The Russians took away many hundreds of the Bombards. When the German soldier encountered the PIAT first in Russia he called it the 'Stuka-zu-Fuß' – the infantry Stuka.

If Whitehall had put the PIAT into production in 1938, as it could well have done, each platoon of that staunch Polish infantry could have had one. It could hardly have failed to smash every one of von Runstedt's tanks. So no Battle of France, or of Holland, or Britain, at all.

BIBLIOGRAPHY

Bailey, Colonel Frederick, *Mission to Tashkent*, Jonathan Cape, 1946

Bush, Vannevar, *Modern Arms and Free Men*, USA, 1949

Crowther, J.G., and Richard Whiddington, *Science at War*, HMSO, 1947

Etherton, Percy, *In the Heart of Asia*, Constable, 1925

Hopkirk, Peter, *Setting the East Ablaze*, John Murray, 1984

Malleson, Major General Sir Wilfred, 'The British Military Mission to Turkestan', *Journal of the Royal Central Asian Society*, Vol. IX, 1922

Sargent, Michael, *British Military Involvement in Transcaspia (1918-1919)*, Conflict Studies Research Centre, April 2004

Teague-Jones, Reginald, *The Spy who disappeared*, Victor Gollancz, 1990

Trevelyan, Raleigh, *The Fortress – A Diary of Anzio & After*, Collins, 1956

Warner, Philip, *The D-Day Landings*, Pen and Sword, 2004

Younghusband, Colonel G. J. *The Story of the Guides*, Macmillan, 1911

INDEX (with notes)

Director of Research Air Ministry 1919-21; Inspector General RAF 1935; C-in-C Far East 1940-41, 65

Bumble, 13, 84

Cammell, Reginald, Lieut RE (1886-1911), the first British military pilot to die in a flying accident, 15, 19

canal tunnel, Malakand, 24, 27, 186

carpentry, 45

cat o' nine tails, 26

cavalry corps, 46

caviar, 102

chemistry, 5

cherry brandy, 35

Cherwell, Frederick Lindemann, Viscount (1886-1957), scientific adviser to Winston Churchill, 187-8

Chichester, Sir Edward, Captain of HMS *Himalaya* in 1894, 2

Churchill, Winston, viii, 168, 176-7, 181, 187
The Hinge of Fate, 187

Clarke, Sir Edmund, 187

Cody, Samuel, flamboyant American aviator who later became British; made Britain's first powered flight in 1908, in his own aeroplane, the *Cathedral*; killed in flying accident 1913, 15

Conneau, Jean (1880-1937), winner of the *Daily Mail* circuit of Britain, of the Paris-Rome air race, and of the European Circuit, all in 1911, 20

Constantinesco, Georges (1881-1965), inventor of the hydraulic gun trigger, 66-7

Conyers, Lt Col Charles, Royal Irish Fusiliers, died 12 May 1915. A tablet to his memory is in the Danish cathedral in Limerick, 8, 9

Cooper, A.C., pilot, Leicestershire Regt, killed in action 1916, 44

Cossacks, 38-40, 68, 79, 101

cotton, gun, 68, note p.104, 186

Cox, Sir Herbert Vaughan (1860-1923), Lt Gen Indian Army in 1917, 19

Crème de menthe, 35, 37

croquet, 5

crucifixion, 24

Cubism and Dadaism, 119

Daily Mail Circuit of Britain, a 24-hour cross-country air race via Edinburgh, Glasgow and Bristol, starting and finishing at Brooklands. Jean Conneau won the $50,000 first prize in 1911. The only British finisher was Samuel Cody (cit.), 20

Dale, Tom, watchmaker, 187

damsels, 87, 119, 127, 140

de Gaulle, 176

Denikin, Gen Anton; in 1919 organized a 60,000-strong White Russian army and attacked the Bolshevik state from the Crimea; the attack failed and he fled to France; died in New York in 1947, 103, 109

devils, brown, 55

Dieppe Raid 1942, 183

Doolittle and Prance, air mechanics, 51

Double Onion, 184

Dowding, Air Chief Marshal Lord (1882-1970), C-in-C Fighter Command 1936-October 40, ('Stuffy'), 46, 53

drill, 6

Dunsterville, Maj Gen Lionel (1865-1946), the model for Stalky in Kipling's *Stalky and Co* (see also Baku), 70, 102

Duncan, Captain, 117, 131, 136

Dunkirk, 174

Dutov, Gen Alexander (1879-1921); in Nov 1917 organized the Dutov revolt against Soviet rule in

Orenburg; led an army against the Bolsheviks in the Urals; when defeated by Red Guards fled to China; assassinated by a Bolshevik agent, 73

Elliott, Harold, 'Trouble', DSO (1878-1931), Australian senator, 187

Etherton, Col Percy (1879-1963), Consul-General Chinese Turkestan 1918-23; Colonel Consul at Kashgar; Hon Sec Houston Mount Everest Flight 1933; pub. *Across the Roof of the World* (1911), 29, 70, 72, 86, 146, 155, 194

Everest, flight over:
American application to fly, 145
astrologers, 155
cameras, 150-3, 155-60
clothing, 157
down-draught, 159
dynamo and electric current, 156, 158
finances, 146, 155, 161-2
fuel, 148-9, 155, 161
lèse-majesté, 146
light, 159
mapping, 148
mental concentration, 156-7
objects of the enterprise, 147
orders departed from, 162
oxygen, 155-6, 159-60
Pegasus aero-engines, 145, 160
permission to fly, 145-7
Royal Geographical Society, 146-7
second flight, 161-2
sound waves, 157
telephone, 157
virgin summit, 146
wind and weather, 155, 160-1
Western Cwm, 147-8

Everest, 1953 ascent of, 147-8

Everest, Sir George (1790-1866), Surveyor General of India 1830-43, 145

exhaustion, and despair, 58-9
experiment, 67

Fedden, Sir Roy (1885-1973), Chief Engineer British Aeroplane Co Ltd. 1920-1942; Special Technical Adviser to Ministry of Aircraft Production 1942-45; pub. *Britain's Air Survival* (1957), 145, 148

fanaticism, Hindustani, 10

Filippi, Count Filippo de (1869-1938), Italian alpinist and explorer; ascended Mount Saint Elias, Alaska; explored Ruwenzori 1906; mountain climbing expedition in Kashmir 1911; geographical expedition in Asia 1914 (his report on this filled sixteen volumes), 30, 32-3, 38

flour, adulterated, 26

flying, training, 16

fog, of war, 58

Fokker, Anthony (1890-1939), aeroplane constructor; contributed to the development of the German version of the synchronized gun, 45, 55, 65, 66, 167

Forsyth, Sir Thomas (1827-1886); his special mission to Kashgar in 1873-74, ostensibly a trade mission, was in fact to counter Russian influence on the Northern Frontier, 29, 36

Frazer-Nash, Archie. His company manufactured sports cars (1905-57) and still exists today as an engineering company, 171

French, Sir John (1852-1925), Earl of Ypres, commander of the British Expeditionary Force which was deployed to France in the opening days of World War One, 46

Ganju Lama VC (1923-2000), 189-90

whose modified tank designs, of
which the Petard was one, played
an important role in the D-Day
landings, **184**, **186**
holes, in fuselage, 53
Holland, General Joe, 174-5
Holland and Holland, 139
Home Guard, **177-8, note p.179**
Hopkinson, Bertram, FRS,
Professor of Applied Mechanics,
Cambridge; Colonel RE; killed
flying, August 1918, 67
Houston, Dame Fanny, DBE
(1857-1936), former chorus girl
whose three wealthy husbands
pre-deceased her; gave £100,000
for the British entry into the
Schneider Cup Contest, and
financed the flight over Everest,
146, **155**, **161-2**, **169**, *25*
Hunza, **27**, **71**, **84**, **91**
human endurance, limit of, 60

ICI, **171**, **175**, **183**, **187-8**
Indian Mutiny, 10
influenza, **90**, **91**
Ismay, General Lionel, DSO
(1887-1965); in the Second World
War was Military Secretary to
the Cabinet and Prime Minister's
representative in the Chiefs of
Staff Committee, **138**, **174**, **178**
Jefferis, Millis, MC (1899-1963),
engineer, head of MIR C, **175**,
187
Jefferson, Francis, VC (1921-82),
189
Jiristan, **131-6**
Jodhpur, 154

Kalbi (Kerbelai Mohammed),
pilgrim and soldier; he believed
that the Revolution was a
punishment to the Russians for
having destroyed the Imam Reza
mosque in Meshed in 1912, **84**,
88-9, **106-7**

Karakorum, **34**
Kathmandu, government, **145**
Khuda Verdi Sardar, 'Khudu', the
problem of, **ch.19**
Kipling, Rudyard, 95
Kirghiz, **36**
Kirkpatrick, Maj-Gen Sir George
(1866-1950), director of military
operations, India 1914-18; Chief of
General Staff, India 1916-20; GOC
forces China 1920-2; GOC western
command India 1923-7, **68**
Kolchak, Admiral Alexandr
(1874-1920), head of anti-
Bolshevik forces in Siberia; later,
dictator in Omsk; killed by firing
squad, **103,110**
Kolesov, railway oiler turned chief
commissar, President of the
Turkestan Republic, **106**

Lama/llama, **71**
Langg-Tai, **87**
Latvia, **140**
Lazarev, General, **115**
Lea, Lt Col George, DSO,
commander 11 Para 1944, 15
Para 1946, 22 SAS in Malaya,
191
Le Mesurier, Col Cecil (1831-1913),
Royal Artillery Afghan War,
designer of the Screw Gun, **165**
Lenin, **139**
Lloyd George, David (1863-1945),
Britain's Prime Minister for the
last two years of World War One,
known as 'the man who won the
War', **167**
Loya, the, **88**
Lutheran colony, **102**
Lutyens, **154**

Macartney, Sir George (1867-1945);
went to Chinese Turkestan with
Younghusband in 1890 to set
up Consulate in Kashgar, and
remained there as Consul General

until 1920; he was half Chinese, 38, 70, 72, 77

Malleson, Maj Gen Sir Wilfred (1866-1945), Head of Intelligence Indian Army HQ 1904-10; Commander East African Expeditionary Force 1915-16; Head of British Military Mission to Turkestan 1918-1920, 70, 77, 104, 114, 194

maps, mapping, 33, 113-4, 126, 135, 148

marmots, 36

Marushka, viii, 100-1

Marxian propaganda, 120-1, 141

massacre, 115, 128, 136, 141

Mazzantini, Luis (1856-1926), the *señorito loco*, celebrated matador of nearly 3,000 bulls, **2**

McFie, Robert, tank designer, **17, 167**

McIntyre, Flt Lt David, second pilot of the Everest expedition; city of Glasgow bomber squadron; co-founder of Prestwick airport, **155**

McNaughton, General Andrew, DSO (1887-1966), GOC First Canadian Division 1939; GOC First Canadian Army 1942-44, **178**

medal, **137**

Milne, Field Marshal George, DSO, Baron of Salonika and Ruslikan (1866-1948), Commander of British-Turkestan operations 1919; CIGS 1926-33, **104, 111**

Mir Dost, Jemadar, 57th Wilde's Rifles; won VC at Ypres for carrying eight officers to safety under very heavy fire; also won the Indian OM, **58**

Mix, Tom, **13**

monocle, **74**

Montgomerie, Thomas George (1838-78), Colonel RE, geographer, **33**

Montgomery, Bernard Law, DSO, Field Marshal Montgomery of El Alamein (1887-1976), **4**

Moore, Sir John (1791-1809), General and tactician who fought and died in the Napoleonic wars; established training and drill regimes for infantry regiments, **6, 163**

mortars, 'Coehorn', **85**

mullahs, **10**

Multan Khan, **10** et seq.

Munroe, Charles (1849-1938), chemist, inventor of smokeless gunpowder and the 'hollow charge' principle, **186**

near miss, **54**

Nepal, **145, 154**

Nicholson, John (1821-57), Commissioner in Peshawur, uncompromising builder of Empire on the Northwest Frontier; was fatally wounded during the aftermath of the Indian Mutiny, **10**

Norway, **143**

oasis, **36**

officialdom, bureaucracy, Whitehall, committees etc, **1, 15, 17, 19, 42, 43, 48, 55, 65, 93, 118, 163-9, 172, 176-8, 180, 182, 193**

Omaha beach, **185**

Omar Khayyam, **113**

Oraz Mahomed, the problem of, **122-5**

Pakenham-Walsh, Maj Gen Ridley, MC (1888-1966), Engineer in Chief for the BEF in France 1939, **57**

Panjdeh Incident 1885, **110**

Parnall Aircraft, **171**

Pasha, Enver (1882-1922), brought Turkey into the war on the side of the Central Powers; his forces took Baku on 14 September 1918 and murdered 15-20,000 Armenians; he lost the city